Historic
SASKATCHEWAN

Historic
SASKATCHEWAN

DEANNA CHRISTENSEN
&
MENNO FIEGUTH

Toronto
OXFORD UNIVERSITY PRESS
1986

Acknowledgements

Our gratitude goes to the many people who welcomed us and provided us with information during our travels through Saskatchewan shooting photographs and collecting research data. Personally, I would like to acknowledge the co-operation I received from staff at various archives and libraries during the past few years, in particular Ian E. Wilson and his colleagues at the Saskatchewan Archives Board and Shirlee Anne Smith and her staff at the Hudson's Bay Company Archives, Provincial Archives of Manitoba. During the writing of this book I appreciated the help of many who willingly answered questions and provided additional information during visits and in response to telephone calls and letters. A special thank you goes to Stewart Raby for reading the manuscript and making suggestions, Barry Ahenakew (Kakisē Watisiwiyin) for his assistance and interest in my work, and Celeste Rider, who lent a hand when I needed it the most. And, as always, I thank Ray Christensen for helping select the photographs, and for his advice, understanding, and patience.

D.C.

CANADIAN CATALOGUING IN PUBLICATION DATA

Christensen, Deanna.
  Historic Saskatchewan

ISBN 0-19-540562-5

1. Saskatchewan — Description and travel — 1981-
Views.* 2. Historic buildings — Saskatchewan —
Pictorial works. 3. Saskatchewan — History — Pictorial
works. I. Fieguth, Menno. II. Title
FC3517.3.C57 1986   971.24'0022'2   C86-094118-3
F1071.C57 1986

Produced by Boulton Publishing Services, Inc.
Designed by Fortunato Aglialoro

1 2 3 4 - 9 8 7 6

Color separations by
Lasersharp Inc., Toronto

Printed in Hong Kong by
Scanner Art Services, Inc., Toronto

INTRODUCTION

If you and I were sitting in a circle of people on the prairie, and if I were then to place a painted drum or an eagle feather in the middle of this circle, each of us would perceive these objects differently. Our vision of them would vary according to our individual positions in the circle, each of which would be unique.

Hyemeyohsts Storm, *Seven Arrows*[1]

And so it should be, for not only do we each occupy a different position in the circle, but the experiences and perspectives we bring to the circle also differ. The Plains Indian philosophy described by Hyemeyohsts Storm has profound implications, for it means that there is no one way of interpreting an event, a thing, or, for that matter, a province. Taken one step further, it means that there is not just 'one' Saskatchewan. There are many.

This collection of photographs and words provides a glimpse of our Saskatchewan, Menno Fieguth's and mine. I met Menno in 1973 at Fort Walsh in the Cypress Hills when he was on a photographic assignment and I was working on a film-strip series. I think this was appropriate, for our 'being there' reflects the approach we have taken to our work since.

Following that visit to the south-western corner of Saskatchewan, Menno and I—each independently—continued to explore the province, he with his camera and I with my paper, pencil, and tape-recorder. Although our perspectives may differ, we share common ground. Both of us were born and raised in Saskatchewan, and both of us know and appreciate the often overlooked diversity of this land and its people. Perhaps most important, we are both fascinated with the 'sense of place'—the feeling that comes from actually being on the site where something 'historic' happened. This feeling makes history come alive.

I experienced this for the first time when I stood on a high bank at the 'forks', overlooking the place where the North and South Saskatchewan rivers flow together. Images of York boats and canoes manned by Indians and voyageurs flashed through my mind, for this was the historic Saskatchewan River, one of the major water highways in North America. From the forks early travellers went east to Hudson Bay or Montréal, west to the Rocky Mountains, or south-west to what is now southern Alberta. I was here, in the twentieth century, but it was exciting to imagine what life must have been like for the people living on this land 150 years ago.

[1]New York, Harper & Row, Publishers, Inc., 1972.

CREE LAKE, NORTHERN SASKATCHEWAN

Sitting in the Hudson's Bay Company Archives reading a journal in the handwriting of a fur trader gives me the same feeling of being there. And I get a similar sensation when an Indian elder talks about his grandfather's experiences hunting buffalo on the plains, or when a woman remembers coming to this land at the turn of the century with parents who were almost penniless and unable to speak English.

In this book we have tried to capture some of the flavour of Saskatchewan, its land, and its people. Photographs are the next best thing to being there, so they have been used to create the framework for developing our look at historic Saskatchewan. Some were taken especially for this volume, while others are the result of journeys through various parts of the province during the past thirteen years. Several of the photographs are historic in themselves. For instance, it is no longer possible to view the Saskatchewan River from the bank where the François-Finlay fur-trade post was situated. The bank and the archaeological remains of the post are now under eighteen metres of water, flooded when the Nipawin Hydroelectric Power Station was constructed. And the pictures of Holy Trinity Anglican Church at Stanley Mission, located in northern Saskatchewan, were taken before restoration was begun in 1981.

Much of the information in the accompanying text has also been collected over a number of years, from archival research and published materials and interviews. Quotations—the actual words of real people—are used in hope that they will inject life and meaning into the times and places captured in the photographs.

Saskatchewan is a land of contrast, a land of change. It can be viewed in many ways, from many perspectives, from many locales. From your position in the circle, we hope you enjoy ours.

DEANNA CHRISTENSEN
Regina, Saskatchewan

ROCK OUTCROPPING NEAR ST. VICTOR—Sculptured and shaped, first by the glaciers of the Ice Age and later by wind, water, heat, and frost, the land that became Saskatchewan is as varied as its history. In the south, rugged outcroppings and wooded uplands rear up from the flat plains. The undulating seas of grass and wheat sweep north, cut occasionally by dramatic river valleys, until they merge with rolling parklands of aspen and birch. And still farther north stretches half a province, consisting of coniferous forests, rivers, lakes, and rock.

The first inhabitants left few physical traces. They were hunters and gatherers, adapting their way of life to suit their environment. Petroglyphs are one of the few remaining signs of these early days. An excellent example of these ancient rock carvings can be found on this sandstone outcropping near St. Victor, approximately 140 kilometres south of Moose Jaw. Reached by a staircase and walkway, the petroglyphs provide a natural beginning for a look at historic Saskatchewan.

PICTOGRAPHS, BETWEEN MARIBELLI AND HICKSON LAKES, NORTHERN SASKATCHEWAN—Pictographs provide a reminder in northern regions that Saskatchewan was occupied long before the Europeans arrived. Unlike the carved petroglyphs at St. Victor, pictographs were painted using a mixture of red ochre and a binding agent such as bear grease or fish oil. Red ochre occurs naturally in the rust-impregnated clay and iron-ore pebbles of the Canadian Shield region, where all of Saskatchewan's known pictographs are located. Rock paintings are associated with Indian religious traditions.

At least sixty-five pictograph sites have been recorded in Saskatchewan, and others, undetected by casual observation, are almost certain to exist. The paintings shown here are located north of Lac la Ronge and the Churchill River.

Fur trader Alexander Mackenzie, in a book telling the story of his journeys to the Arctic and Pacific oceans in 1789 and 1793, provides what may be the first written account of pictographs in Saskatchewan. He wrote that in a narrow strait along Churchill River they passed a place

where the Indians have painted red figures on the face of a rock, and where it was their custom formerly to make an offering of some of the articles which they had with them, in [sic] their way to and from the Churchill.

ST. VICTOR'S PETROGLYPHS *(left)*—On a clear day, when the sun is low, petroglyphs of grizzly bear tracks and the prints of clovenhoofed animals such as bison, deer, elk, and antelope can be seen on the top of the sandstone cliff near St. Victor. Other rock carvings include turtles, and human heads, footprints, and hand prints. The word petroglyph comes from a combination of *petros*, the Greek word for 'rock', and *glupho*, meaning 'I cut or carve.'

The outcropping at St. Victor is believed to have been a holy place where Indian people fasted and prayed. Although it is not known when the carvings were made, horse hoofs are not included. This likely means that the figures were created before the horse was introduced to the northern plains in the early 1700s. Many of the carvings are superimposed on each other, suggesting that the panorama of petroglyphs took form over many years.

The carvings of St. Victor, now part of a provincial park, are unusual in being located on the top surface of the rocks rather than on a vertical face. At least sixteen other prehistoric petroglyph sites have been recorded in Saskatchewan. They are all of the 'vertical face' type and were found in the prairie-parkland region. Six of these have been removed from their original site.

DRINKING FALLS, CHURCHILL RIVER—Instead of following a direct course, the Churchill River is a vast maze of island-studded lakes connected by channels of swift-flowing white water. The name of the stretch of white water shown here, situated east of Lac la Ronge, was officially changed from Drinking Falls to Potter Rapids in 1955.

Archaeological evidence indicates that the Churchill River region was occupied by Woods Cree as early as the tenth century. They supported themselves by hunting woodland caribou, moose, and other game during the winter, and by fishing and hunting geese and ducks in the summer. After the Hudson's Bay Company established fur-trade posts on the shores of Hudson Bay in the seventeenth century, the Cree started harvesting furs to exchange for European trade goods.

At first they made the long trip to Hudson Bay or else traded with Indian middle men. Then fur traders from Montréal and Hudson Bay moved inland. By the 1770s rival traders were building competing posts at strategic locations along the Churchill River as they battled for supremacy of the fur trade.

Without Indian guides the first White explorers and fur traders would have faced an almost impossible task in following this river of rapids, innumerable channels, and undulating shoreline. One trader counted as many as thirty-six places where canoes and boats had to be carried, or portaged, around sections of the river that were too wild for canoe travel. Whirlpools also presented a hazard. Mackenzie described one place that was

improperly called a lake [Black Bear Island Lake], as it contains frequent impediments amongst its islands, from rapids. There is a very dangerous one about the centre of it, which is named the Rapids qui ne parle point, or that never speaks, from its silent whirlpool-motion. In some of the whirlpools the suction is so powerful, that they are carefully avoided.

PORTAGE LA LOCHE—After a gruelling trip up the Churchill River, working against the current and carrying loads around turbulent, frothing rapids, canoemen reached the relatively quiet waters of Lac La Loche.

This lake—and the rivers and streams that feed into it—marks the extreme north-western end of the Churchill watershed, where the Churchill River begins.

Beyond Lac La Loche a height of land separates the Churchill River watershed from that of the Athabasca. On the south side of this ridge, water drains into the Churchill system, eventually emptying into Hudson Bay far to the east. North of the ridge the rivers and streams flow into Lake Athabasca, which in turn drains into Great Slave Lake and the Arctic Ocean.

In 1778 Peter Pond and his party of voyageurs were taken over the height of land by Indian guides, making Pond the first White man to travel from the Churchill River to the watershed of the Athabasca. The nineteen-kilometre route over which the canoes were carried became known as Portage La Loche. For part of this century the portage and lake bore the name 'Methy', but in the 1950s each was officially given back its original designation.

When Alexander Mackenzie traversed Portage La Loche in the late 1790s, he described the height of land as

a very steep precipice, whose ascent and descent appears to be equally impracticable in any way, as it consists of a succession of eight hills, some of which are almost perpendicular; nevertheless, the Canadians [voyageurs] contrive to surmount all these difficulties, even with their canoes and lading.

When they reached the northern end of the portage *(overleaf)*, the fur traders found themselves on the banks of the Clearwater River. The river is visible beyond the frames that are used for smoking and stretching hides.

CLEARWATER RIVER *(above)*—By crossing Portage La Loche, the fur traders opened up new areas to exploration and trade. The Clearwater River led to the Lake Athabasca region. From there routes extended north to the Arctic Ocean and west to the Continental Divide and the Pacific Ocean. This vast land of forests, rivers, and lakes—and the country beyond—was one of the richest fur-bearing areas in the world. North West Company trader Daniel Harmon, who made his first trip across Portage La Loche in 1808, described the view as he looked north:

Two lofty and extensive ridges, enclose a valley, about three miles in width, which stretches, far as the eye can reach. The Little River... winds, in a most delightful manner, along this charming valley... on the whole, the most delightful, natural scenery, that I ever beheld.

Although this area was first occupied by the Woods Cree, the lure of the fur trade drew the Dene from their northern homeland of transitional forest and tundra to the Churchill and Athabasca districts. These Dene were called Chipewyan by the Cree and subsequent fur traders. Before the inland posts were built, the Dene dealt with middle men or made the long journey to trade at Prince of Wales's Fort (Fort Churchill) on the shores of Hudson Bay.

The Clearwater River, in recognition of its natural, historical, and recreational features, is the first river in Saskatchewan to become part of the Canadian Heritage River System.

PORTAGE LA LOCHE *(left)*

CREE LAKE — By 1790 the Dene had started their southern expansion and were occupying an area that extended just beyond Cree Lake. The lake is east of the Clearwater River; at that time it was within the southern limits of the traditional wintering range of the barren-ground caribou. Before the Dene became extensively involved in the fur trade, this migratory species of caribou provided food, tools, hides, and practically everything else needed for survival.

According to Samuel Hearne, a Hudson's Bay fur trader and explorer who travelled extensively in the far northern regions during the 1770s, the Dene's method of hunting caribou with log enclosures called pounds was

sometimes so successful, that many families subsist by it without having occasion to move their tents above once or twice during the course of a whole winter... The real wants of these people are few, and easily supplied: a hatchet, an ice-chissel [sic], a file, and a knife, are all that is required to enable them, with a little industry, to procure a comfortable livelihood.

THE SASKATCHEWAN RIVER, NEAR NIPAWIN—The Cree nicknamed it *Kici Sipi*, 'Great River'. More formally, it was called *Kākisiskātchewan Sipi*, 'Swift Flowing River'. With the arrival of the European fur traders, the river that became known as the 'Saskatchewan' developed into a major water highway, linking the plains and parklands of the North-West with York Factory on the shores of Hudson Bay and Montréal on the St. Lawrence River.

The French were the first to establish posts along its banks. Following the fall of New France to the British in 1760, the French fur empire was taken over by independent traders who became known as 'Pedlars'; some of these men eventually formed the North West Company. In 1768 François Le Blanc, a man in his sixties who had been associated with the French traders for nearly thirty years, joined forces with Scotchman James Finlay to establish one of the first Pedlar posts in what is now Saskatchewan. It was located to the right of the bank shown in this photograph.

The voyageurs and boatmen responsible for transporting freight up the Saskatchewan likely used more colourful (and less printable!) words than swift flowing to describe this river. From below Nipawin to the forks, a distance of 200 kilometres, paddling was impossible as men battled rapids and strong currents. Nor'Wester Duncan M'Gillivray wrote in 1794 that

this part of the River is an object of terror... The usual mode of navigation is here rendered useless by the Strength of the Current, which makes it necessary to haul the Canoes up along Shore with a line, for that purpose, for the space of 6 days on an exceeding bad Road.

According to Alexander Henry the younger, to accomplish this,

two men remained on board to keep the canoe straight, while the four middlemen [went ashore and] tackled themselves to the towing-line by means of their portage-slings... All hands... [then] march on a round trot, through mud and mire and over loose stones, [thereby pulling the loaded canoe up the river].

The site of the François-Finlay complex was part of the area flooded in the fall of 1985 to create the reservoir at the Nipawin Hydroelectric Project. It is now covered by eighteen metres of water. The dam has been named the François-Finlay Dam.

POWDER HOUSE, CUMBERLAND HOUSE—Faced with competition from the Pedlars, the Hudson's Bay Company abandoned its policy of waiting at York Factory for the Indians to arrive with furs, and in 1774 Samuel Hearne built Cumberland House on the Saskatchewan River delta near the present-day Saskatchewan–Manitoba border. This was the first fur-trade post built by the company in the interior of the North-West.

Hearne and his party of men travelled to Saskatchewan River country with several groups of Indians. After exploring the area for nearly three weeks, the Hudson's Bay officer wrote in his journal that

after a long Consultation with the Indian Chiefs and others in Company, I determine'd to build the [fur trade] house, at least for the insewing [sic] winter at a Part Call'd Pine Island Lake— it is the general opinion of those Indians that that part will be

more comodious [sic] both for Drawing the Indians to trade as well as for Provisions than Basquiau [The Pas]...

The post was built on Pine Island. It proved to be extremely well located, sitting at the hub of routes leading south-west to the buffalo plains, north-west to the fur-rich Churchill and Athabasca regions, and east to York Factory. It consequently served as a transportation and distribution centre during most of the fur-trade era.

In the 1790s the Hudson's Bay post was relocated to another part of Pine Island. The community that developed nearby formed the nucleus of Saskatchewan's first permanent settlement. In 1886 the thick-walled stone powder house shown here was built by the company to replace one in poor repair. It is now part of a provincial historic park on the edge of the community of Cumberland House.

FORT CARLTON—Fort Carlton was one of the great pemmican posts in the Canadian North-West. Built in 1810 by the Hudson's Bay Company on the banks of the North Saskatchewan River, some eighty kilometres upstream from present-day Prince Albert, the post was so well located that it remained in operation on the same flat of land until 1885. This was very unusual in the Saskatchewan River trade; companies continually moved posts to gain an advantage with Indian hunters and trappers.

In the woodlands within the post's trading area, the Cree trapped small fur-bearing animals such as beaver, fisher, and marten, and they hunted elk, moose, and deer. The Indians from the plains, primarily Cree and Assiniboine, brought in muskrat, wolf, and fox. But it was the buffalo, which migrated between the parkland and the prairies, that provided the main rationale for Fort Carlton's existence. The great buffalo herds often were so close that they ate the stacks of hay stored near the post.

Buffalo meat was dried, pounded into shreds, and mixed with fat (and sometimes berries) to make pemmican. Because it was concentrated, light in weight, and nutritious, and kept well, pemmican was an ideal food to distribute to the men transporting furs and trade goods between the posts and the main depots. As traders travelled farther and farther west and north-west in their quest for furs, pemmican became the lifeline of the fur trade.

Some years Fort Carlton collected vast amounts of buffalo meat and other provisions from the plains. For instance, during the 1813–14 trading season, 64,851 pounds of fresh buffalo meat, 1,366 pounds of dried meat, 800 pounds of fat, and 1,200 pounds of pemmican were eaten by the twenty-four men, the officers, and women and children at the post. That same season Fort Carlton collected 1,465 pounds of dried meat, 1,120 pounds of fat, and 9,670 pounds of pemmican for the general transportation system. But not all years were ones of plenty. When the buffalo stayed away, the traders went hungry and sometimes almost starved.

12 RED RIVER CART WHEEL, FORT CARLTON—Fort Carlton was strategically located for transportation and buffalo hunting. The post was on a major water highway at a place known as 'the crossing', where an overland shortcut between the North and South Saskatchewan rivers crossed the North Branch. This trail eventually became part of the Carlton Trail; it started at Fort Garry (Winnipeg) and extended north-west to Fort Carlton and beyond to Fort Pitt and Fort Edmonton.

During the 1860s the Hudson's Bay Company started freighting some trade goods by ox cart on the Carlton Trail, instead of bringing everything by boat from York Factory. Long trains of Red River carts squealed across the plains to Fort Carlton. From there freight was directed to points farther north and west, making the post on the North Saskatchewan an important transportation and distribution centre. It also became a meeting place for travellers in the North-West.

In 1862 John McDougall, who was nineteen at the time, arrived at Fort Carlton by boat and waited at the post for his Methodist missionary father, George, to arrive by horseback from Fort Garry. The younger McDougall followed in his father's footsteps and later served as a missionary in Alberta. He described some of the activities at Fort Carlton during his 1862 visit:

The old fort and the plain around was a busy scene—our crews from the boats, hunters from the plains, parties of Indians in to trade, the air full of stories about the southern Indians and the tribal wars to and fro ... The herds of buffalo [were] said to be within a hundred miles from the fort, or less than two days out. Buffalo-skin lodges and canvas tents dotted the plain in every direction. Horse-races and foot-races were common occurrences. I championed older Canada against Indians, half-breeds and Hudson's Bay officials and employees, and in the foot-racing and jumping—high, long, and hop, step and jump—'cleaned out the crowd' and made a name for myself and country.

Fort Carlton accidentally caught fire while steps were being taken to evacuate it during the first stages of the 1885 uprising. It was partially rebuilt during the 1960s and is now a provincial historic park.

THICKWOOD HILLS—Winter brought new patterns to life in the North-West. As part of a seasonal cycle, the buffalo travelled north from the plains into the parklands. The Indian people, anticipating this shift, moved too, setting up camps in the river valleys and wooded areas where there was protection from the wind and an abundance of firewood. In a hunting method used almost exclusively in the fall and winter months, enclosures called pounds were built from logs and brush. The buffalo were driven into them and killed with relative ease. Winter was also the time for trapping, when pelts of fur-bearing animals were thick and luxurious. The Thickwood Hills were well known for their abundance of beaver and other fine furs—so much so, in fact, that there are numerous references in early fur-trade records to trading houses being built on the 'track' of the Woods Cree who lived in the Thickwood Hills.

Life at fur-trade posts during the winter months became a monotonous routine of cutting and transporting firewood, hauling wood, cleaning snow out of the fort yard, and doing daily chores. Indian and half-breed hunters were usually hired to hunt, and men were assigned to haul meat by dog sled from the hunting camps. Rather than waiting for Indians to come to the post, small expeditions were sent to the camps to trade for furs, buffalo meat, and pemmican. For the women at the post, as always, it was a time for sewing, cleaning, cooking, and caring for the children.

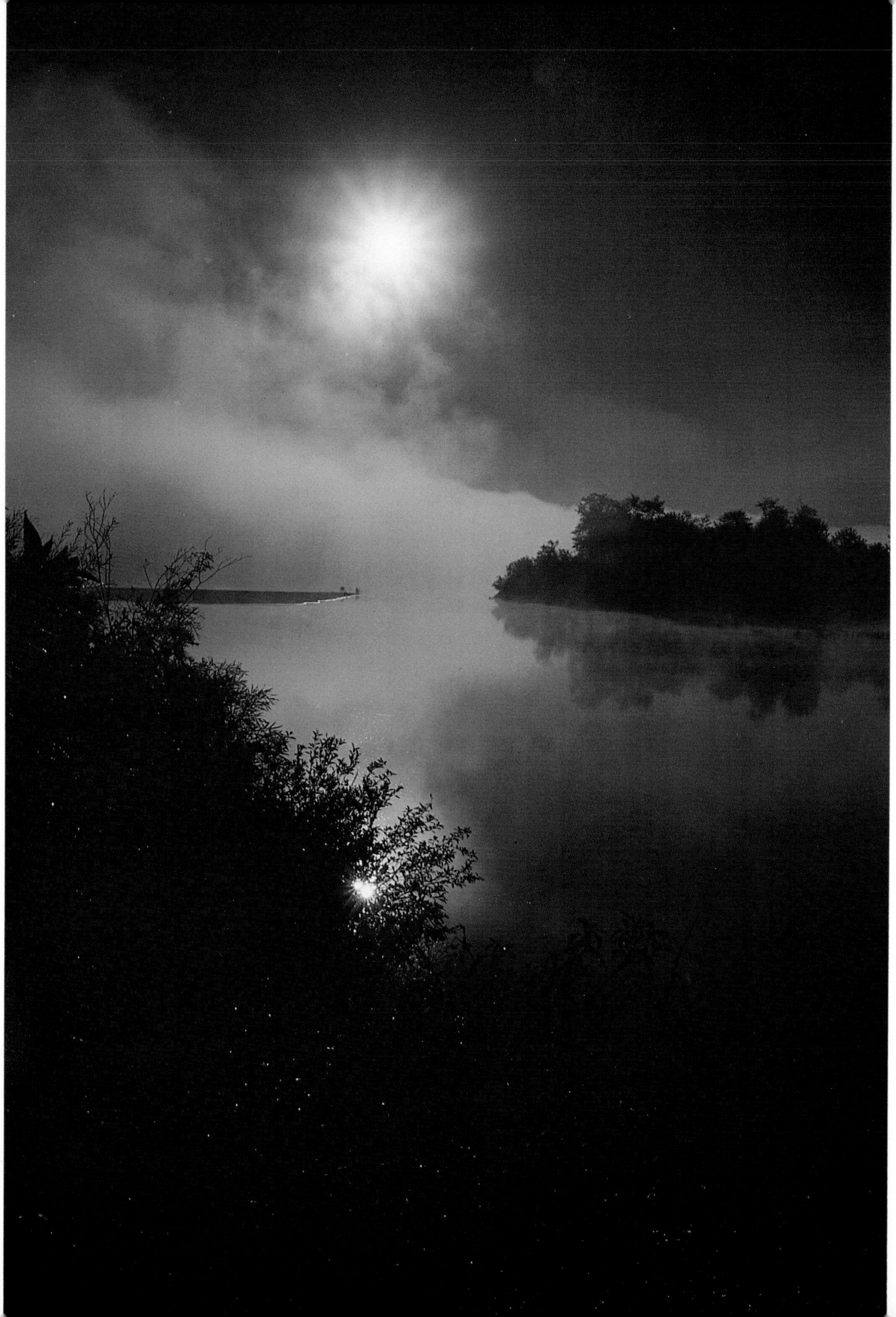

REMAINS OF THE *NORTHCOTE*, CUMBERLAND HOUSE—The *Northcote*, the first steamboat to ply the waters of the Saskatchewan River, was beached for the final time at Cumberland House in 1886. Her wooden superstructure was eventually burned by the Hudson's Bay officer at Cumberland House to prevent young people from playing inside the boat. Only a few pieces of wood, the boilers, and other metal pieces survived. Although most of the wood has since disappeared, the boilers and part of the paddle-wheel are now part of an interpretive display at the provincial historic park at Cumberland House.

The *Northcote*'s beginnings were more grandiose than her ending. The stern-wheeler was launched from Grand Rapids at the mouth of the Saskatchewan River, 330 kilometres east of Cumberland House, on 1 August 1874. She reached the Indian settlement and Anglican mission at The Pas on the 26th. The Rev. Henry Budd, an ordained Swampy Cree minister in charge of the mission, enthusiastically recorded the arrival:

The long expected steamer 'North-Cote' came puffing up in sight. They blew the whistle so loud they made the very cattle rear up their heels, and took to full gallop with their tails up in the air in full speed to the woods. But, not only the cattle but the people of all ages and sexes were no less excited at the sight of the boat, the first boat of the kind to be seen by them all their life; in fact, the first steam boat going in this river since the Creation.

The excitement remained, but the brief era of steamboats on the Saskatchewan proved a frustrating one. The river's shallow water, boulders, shifting sand-bars, and rapids all made navigation difficult. Perhaps the Edmonton *Bulletin* described the situation best when it noted on 5 November 1881 that 'the Saskatchewan is considered by some not to be fit for navigation but it must be very bad indeed if it is not better than slow going oxen on a muddy road one thousand miles long.'

CONFLUENCE OF THE NORTH SASKATCHEWAN AND BATTLE RIVERS *(left)*—Attention focused on the Saskatchewan River each spring and fall. As soon as the ice was gone and the water navigable, the furs and provisions collected at the posts during the winter were loaded onto boats or canoes. The Hudson's Bay Company officers delivered their cargo to York Factory for shipment to England, whereas the North West Company transported its harvest to Montréal via Grand Portage. This inland depot was located at the western end of Lake Superior.

Trade goods for the upcoming season were then loaded onto the boats and canoes for the return journey. The Saskatchewan River traders usually arrived at their posts in late August or early September, where they were welcomed home by their families and the skeleton staff that had remained behind.

16 LAST MOUNTAIN HOUSE—The Hudson's Bay Company was operating successfully in the eastern part of what is now Saskatchewan as early as the 1790s. By the middle of the following century, posts in this area included Fort Pelly on the Assiniboine River, Fort Qu'Appelle on the Qu'Appelle River, and Fort Ellice at the junction of the Assiniboine and Qu'Appelle rivers in present-day Manitoba. Good-quality furs were plentiful, and the buffalo herds were close enough to provide adequate provisions. By the 1860s, however, the massive herds were dwindling in size and retreating farther south and west. In order to obtain buffalo meat and pemmican, trading houses were established farther out on the plains closer to the buffalo and the Indians who were hunting them. One of these posts was Last Mountain House, built in 1869 near the south end of Last Mountain Lake as an outpost of Fort Qu'Appelle.

Isaac Cowie, a twenty-one-year-old apprentice clerk from the Orkney Islands, was put in charge of Last Mountain House. Second in command was Joseph McKay, a half-breed officer from a well-known fur-trade family.

Although McKay moved his family to Last Mountain House and made the post his home base, the veteran trader spent most of the winter travelling to Indian camps to trade. This was necessary in order to compete with the free traders from the United States and the Red River settlement, near what today is Winnipeg, who were working in the area.

When Cowie arrived at Last Mountain House in November 1869, he found the post partly completed:

The buildings . . . were arranged in the usual manner on three sides of a square . . . The stores on the south side and the row of men's houses on the north side were finished, but the master's house [the building with windows], which Joe and family and I were to occupy, was roofless and floorless still.

The building was finished, and Cowie spent a relatively uneventful season at the post. The following year the buffalo hunt failed in the district, and Last Mountain House was apparently closed. It has been partially rebuilt as a provincial historic park.

FORT QU'APPELLE *(above and overleaf)*—The provisions and furs collected at Last Mountain House were sent by Red River cart and dog sled to Fort Qu'Appelle. From there they were carted to Fort Pelly for transport by boat to York Factory via the Swan and Nelson rivers.

Fort Qu'Appelle, established in 1864, was erected between two lakes in the Qu'Appelle Valley. The two buildings shown here are original structures and represent two different eras of Hudson's Bay Company trade. The small white house was part of the fur-trade post built near the river joining the two lakes. The brick-fronted building, with side and back walls made of stone, was a commercial store erected at the turn of the century. It was built on a street in the town of Fort Qu'Appelle that developed near the old fur-trade post. This store marks the transition of the Hudson's Bay Company from trading for furs to merchandising products for the new settler population.

The old 'Bay' store, with its original façade and period windows, has recently been designated provincial heritage property and is to be preserved by a private developer.

According to Cowie, in the 1860s the buildings at Fort Qu'Appelle were made from squared logs and 'thickly thatched with beautiful yellow straw—the best roof to keep in heat as well as to keep it out that I have ever lived under'. They were enclosed by a forty-six-metre-square stockade. Only two buildings had glass windows; buffalo parchment was stretched across the window openings of the others. Only the officers' quarters had iron stoves. In the other living quarters, immense, open fireplaces 'all made of mud' were used for heating and cooking. The fire also provided light, because 'tallow was too much in demand in making of pemmican to permit of its being used luxuriously in making candles merely to light "the men's houses".'

The buildings used for storage and trading were not heated, nor did they have a chimney, for

the fear of fire in a fort where gunpowder was the chief article kept for trade was too great to permit of even the trading shop being heated in the coldest day in winter. This was the rule all over the country, and the men who defied the intense cold when travelling in the open used to dread the more intense cold which seemed to accumulate in the trading store, where one had to spend hours at a stretch writing down each item as the band of Indians brought in their credit slips from the master's office.

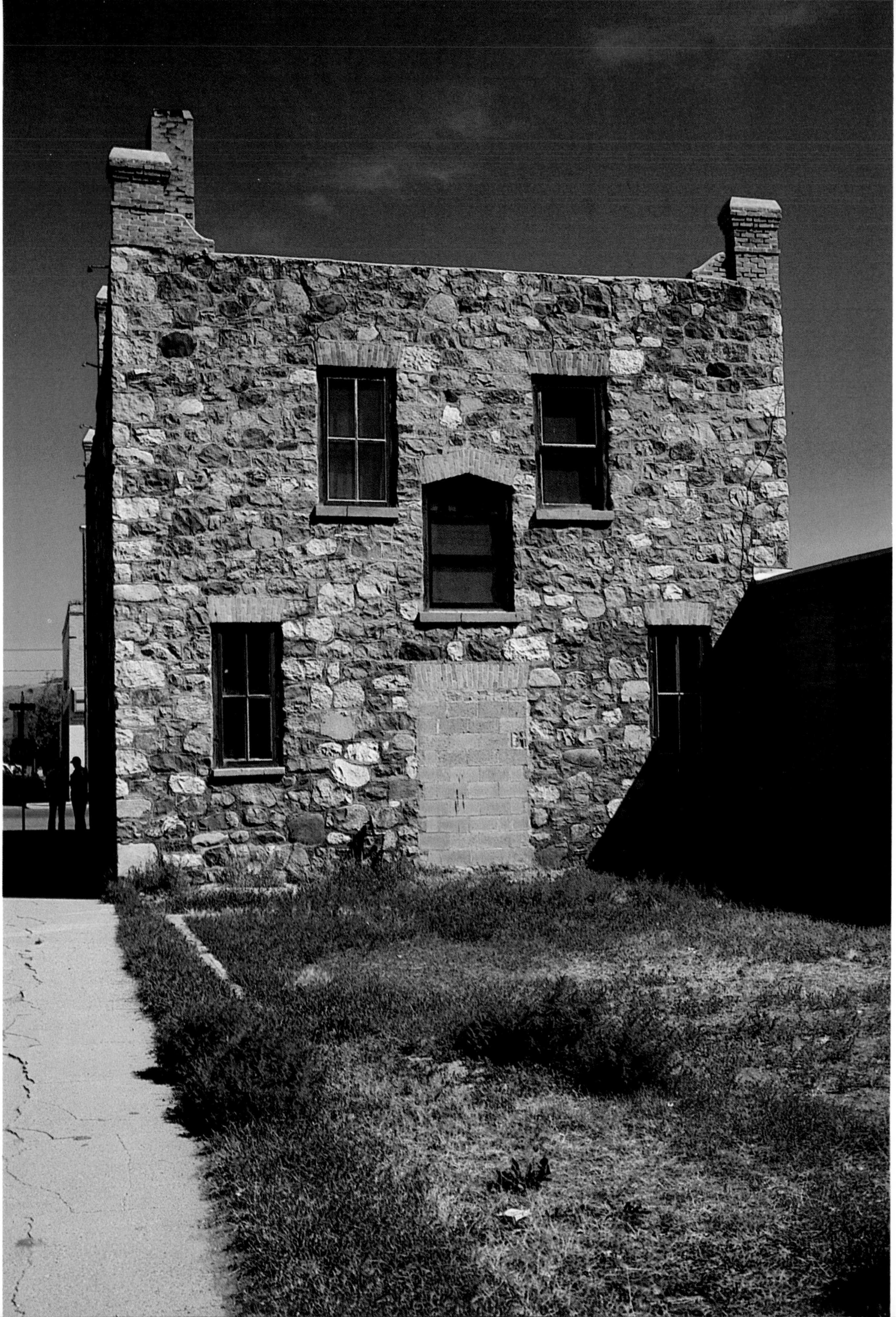

KATEPWA LAKE, QU'APPELLE VALLEY—Many years ago a young Indian man set off on a journey to test his bravery and prove he was worthy of claiming the daughter of a great chief as his wife. His venture was successful, but when the warrior returned, he discovered that the chief's band had moved up river. Borrowing a birch-bark canoe, the brave young man paddled in search of the camp. Darkness came, but still he paddled on. Suddenly he heard a voice calling from the woods. The young man cried out, *Awina Katēpwet*, 'Who is calling?' There was no answer, so he continued his journey. Three times he heard the voice, and three times he responded. And still there was no reply.

When the warrior reached the camp, he was told that the chief's daughter had died during the night. Just before she died the girl said his name three times and called for him to come quickly to her. The young man told the gathering about the voice he had heard, and they knew that the maiden's spirit had gone to the woods and would remain there until after the body was buried, when it was time to enter the spirit world. The young warrior said his farewells and travelled back to the place where he had heard the voice. There he drowned himself so his spirit could accompany the spirit of his loved one into the other world. Henceforth, the Indian people called this river *Awina Katēpwew Sipi*, the 'Who Calls River'.

When Nor'Wester Daniel Harmon reached the river in 1804, he was told that the natives 'imagine a Spirit is constantly going up and down the River, and its voice they say they often hear, but it resembles the cry of a human being'. French-speaking fur traders translated 'Who Calls' into their own language, and the name of the river and its valley became Qu'Appelle.

This lake, the most easterly in a chain of four in the Qu'Appelle Valley, carries a derivative of the Cree name, Katepwa.

20 SOUTH SASKATCHEWAN RIVER VALLEY—So many buffalo once roamed the prairies that their numbers are almost unimaginable. With estimates exceeding sixty million, it is not surprising that the Rev. Robert Rundle, a Methodist missionary, was prompted to write in 1846 that the buffalo 'were in numbers—numberless'. In 1865 John McDougall came across 'a large round plain, perhaps ten miles across...It did not seem possible to pack another buffalo into the space. The whole prairie was one dense mass.' Some two years later Isaac Cowie told of encountering a massive herd north-west of Last Mountain Lake:

Our route took us into the midst of the herd, which opened in front and closed behind the train of carts like water around a ship... The earth trembled day and night, as they moved...

over the undulations of the plains but always leaving an open space about the width of the range of an Indian gun in our front, rear and flanks.

The buffalo provided the fresh and dried meat, pemmican, fat, and other products necessary to sustain the fur trade. For the Indian people of the plains, the buffalo gave the gift of independence. According to Nor'Wester Daniel Harmon in an entry in his 1804 journal,

Those Indians who reside in the large Plains are the most independent and appear to be the happiest and most contented of any People upon the face of the Earth. They subsist on the Flesh of the Buffaloe [sic] and of their Skins they make the greatest part of their Cloathing [sic], which is both warm and convenient.

CHIMNEY COULEE—For many years the Métis from the Red River Settlement made two buffalo hunts each year to obtain provisions for the settlement and the Hudson's Bay Company. Well organized and conducted under strict regulations called the 'law of the prairie', the buffalo hunts of the Métis became famous. As the demand for pemmican, buffalo robes, and other buffalo produce grew, longer and longer lines of screeching, squealing Red River carts etched trails westward. It is said that in 1840, 1,210 carts, accompanied by 620 hunters, 650 women, 360 children, 403 'buffalo runner' horses, 655 cart horses, and 586 draught oxen, left Red River to take part in the summer hunting expedition.

As the buffalo withdrew farther west and south, the distances the Métis had to travel became greater, and it was increasingly difficult for them to return home each winter. Many chose to spend the winter in small groups at sheltered places such as Chimney Coulee, Wood Mountain, Touchwood Hills, the Qu'Appelle Valley, and St. Laurent.

In the fall of 1871 Isaac Cowie and a group of Métis hired by the Hudson's Bay Company built a small post near independent Métis hunters at Chimney Coulee. Located at the eastern edge of the Cypress Hills in what is now south-western Saskatchewan, this locale had been a wintering place for Métis hunters since the 1850s.

During the course of the season, Cowie collected 750 grizzly bear skins and 1,500 elk hides, in addition to furs and provisions. The Hudson's Bay trader was, however, unable to establish a friendly relationship with the Blackfoot who frequented the area, and they burned the buildings immediately after he left. The post was not reopened.

BULL'S FOREHEAD—This impressive land formation is located at the junction of the South Saskatchewan and Red Deer rivers, immediately east of the present-day Saskatchewan–Alberta boundary. The first fur-trade posts in the area were built near Bull's Forehead in 1800. The region was then inhabited by Gros Ventre Indians and Indian bands from the Blackfoot Confederacy.

The traders came from three competing firms: the Hudson's Bay and North West companies and a new trading concern called the XY Company. Uncertain of their reception in a region inhabited by plains tribes that had a reputation for being extremely independent and self-sufficient, the Hudson's Bay men and the Nor'Westers built their posts within a common stockade. The XY traders

erected a house nearby. The Hudson's Bay post, under the command of Peter Fidler, was called Chesterfield House.

The following season only the Hudson's Bay and XY Companies were located near Bull's Forehead. Within six days of his arrival, Fidler reported that 'not less than 14 hundred men women and children...belonging to the 3 tribes [Blackfoot, Blood, and Gros Ventre]' were camped near the post. Before long there were 'millions of buffalo' in sight.

The posts were abandoned in the spring of 1802. The entire region remained free of traders, with the exception of the 1804–05 and 1822–23 seasons, until the 1860s when traders moved into the Cypress Hills farther to the south.

GREAT SAND HILLS (right)—Although the usual image of Saskatchewan's Great Sand Hills mirrors the extensive stretches of shifting sand illustrated here, active dunes represent only a very small portion of the area. The rest of the sand has become anchored by native grasses, cacti, shrubs, and sage-brush. Small clumps of aspen, birch, and willow grow in the lower stabilized areas. The ripples are caused by the wind and are formed at right angles to its prevailing direction.

The Great Sand Hills are south-east of Bull's Forehead and are bordered by the South Saskatchewan River on the north and the Trans-Canada Highway on the south. The area is home to some of the largest populations of mule deer and sharp-tailed grouse in Saskatchewan. For several thousand years prior to their extinction, buffalo roamed this area in immense herds.

James Macoun, a naturalist who made a number of

early surveys of the North-West, travelled through the southern reaches of the Great Sand Hills in 1880. He described 'high hills of sand, that were constantly changing both shape and position by the action of the winds'. In the midst of these hills of sand Macoun found

numerous small groves, and in one place a perfect oasis of nearly 700 acres, covered with large trees, brushwood, ponds, and fine meadows... completely surrounded by sand hills... Numerous ponds of fresh water lay along the base of the sand hills, but not a drop of any description was found on the plain to the south.

Archaeological and historical evidence indicates that Indian people have been hunting and camping in the Great Sand Hills since 9000 B.C. During historic times, Indian peoples frequenting the area have included the Gros Ventre, Blackfoot, Assiniboine, and Plains Cree.

CYPRESS HILLS—Rising 1,466 metres above sea-level, the Cypress Hills have the distinction of being the highest point of land in Canada between Labrador and the Rocky Mountains. They are enough of an oddity that some describe this beautiful plateau extending from the far south-western corner of Saskatchewan into Alberta as 'the hills that shouldn't be'. The geological process that made the Cypress Hills different had its beginnings some forty or fifty million years ago when streams originating in the Rocky Mountains flowed through the area, laying down a bed of round cobble-stones, sand, and gravel. Millions of years passed. The streams dried up, and the deep layer of sediments cemented together to form a tough conglomerate that made an erosion-resistant cap. The surrounding terrain, made of softer materials, gradually eroded away until it lay at a much lower level. What had once been river beds and flood plains was now a flat-topped plateau some 457 metres higher than the plains below. The conglomerate formation, as illustrated here, is exposed at a number of locations.

The plateau was high enough to be only thinly covered by glaciers during the Ice Age, with some parts escaping the ice completely. As a result the Cypress Hills are a gold-

mine for palaeontologists seeking fossils. Among the significant finds have been dinosaur fossils seventy million years old and skeletal remains of mammals who lived during the Oligocene epoch forty million years ago. The Oligocene fossils are the only ones of this age found in Canada; they include bones from Titanothere, a rhinoceros-like animal with a unique branched horn on its nose. Other remains include a hornless rhinoceros, and members of the deer and pig families.

The beauty and uniqueness of the Cypress Hills did not pass unnoticed by scientists who assisted with the earliest surveys of the North-West. Geologist James Hector, twenty-three years old when he accompanied John Palliser on his scientific expedition of the North-West in the late 1850s, wrote that he 'left the Cypress Hills with much regret, as it promised to be one of the most interesting spots in the country'. Some years later, botanist John Macoun stated, 'In all my wandering I never saw any spot to equal in beauty the central plateau of the Cypress Hills.' Macoun accurately predicted that the Cypress Hills and their surroundings would eventually be some of the best ranching country in the North-West.

FARWELL'S TRADING POST, CYPRESS HILLS—In the fall of 1872, Abel Farwell and Moses Solomon, independent traders working out of Fort Benton in Montana, occupied small trading houses on opposite sides of the Battle River in the Cypress Hills. They were only two of a number of American traders who set up posts in Canadian territory during the early 1870s. Although well-stocked posts carried the usual trade items, such as tea, tobacco, ammunition, kettles, and cloth, doctored-up whisky and other concoctions were high-profit items often unscrupulously bartered with Indian customers. These fiery mixtures were made from various combinations of alcohol, water, tobacco, red pepper, Jamaica ginger, molasses, red ink, bluestone, and whatever else was handy. The traders became known as whisky traders, and some of their forts acquired names that reflected their unsavoury character: Whoop-Up, Whiskey Gap, and Standoff. These traders were probably more interested in buffalo hides than they were in furs, since the hides were in demand in the eastern United States for making belts to run industrial machines.

The Farwell and Solomon posts had less evocative names than the Alberta ones, but they were of the same mould. Their customers included the Cree, Saulteaux, and Assiniboine bands who were being drawn to the Cypress Hills in their quest for the buffalo that had disappeared from eastern and northern plains. This intrusion into an area that had been considered either neutral ground or enemy territory was an indication of the traumatic changes taking place in the North-West. Eventually these changes would bring an end to a traditional way of life.

VIEW FROM BALD BUTTE, CYPRESS HILLS *(left)*— Like an island in a sea of grass, the Cypress Hills overlook the plains that spread north. For the members of the Palliser expedition and other travellers, the Cypress Hills were an oasis with plentiful supplies of wood, water, deer, antelope, elk, moose, and other game. The first White men to visit the area were likely the traders from Chesterfield House and the other posts built at the junction of the South Saskatchewan and Red Deer rivers in 1800. These men were taken to the hills by Blackfoot guides to collect pitch from the pines for waterproofing their canoes.

The French-Canadian voyageurs thought the lodgepole pine growing on the plateau were the jack pine or 'cypre' that grew in eastern Canada, and they misnamed the hills the *Montagne de Cyprè*, which in English became Cypress Hills. The Cree had a more accurate and picturesque name, *Minata kawa*, the 'hilly with patches of bushes area'.

Traditionally the Cypress Hills were considered to be a no-man's land between enemy Indian nations. According to Cowie, who first visited the area in 1868,

As far back as the memory and traditions of the Crees then living extended, these Cypress Hills...had been neutral ground between many different warring tribes, south of the newly marked international boundary, as well as the Crees and the Blackfeet and their friends. No Indian for hunting purposes ever set foot on the hills, whose wooded coulees and ravines became the undisturbed haunt of all kinds of game... Only wary and watchful war parties of any tribe ever visited the hills, and so dangerous was it to camp in them that it was customary for such parties to put up barricades about the spots on which they stayed over night.

FARWELL'S POST, SITE OF CYPRESS HILLS MASSA-
CRE—In late May 1873, thirty tipis of Assiniboine led by
Little Soldier, thirteen tipis belonging to Little Chief's
band, and several smaller groups of Indians were camped
in the coulee near Farwell's post. Although minor distur-
bances had flared, there were no unmanageable problems
until a gang of about twelve wolf hunters arrived. The
wolfers, who poisoned wolves by sprinkling strychnine on
buffalo carcasses, had been looking for forty horses presumably stolen by Cree raiders near Fort Benton. They
were assured that the horses were not in the Assiniboine
camp. However, when a Farwell employee discovered
during a drinking bout on 1 June that one of his horses was
missing, tempers erupted. The Indians were warned by
two Métis at the post that a dangerous situation was
developing.

The women and children fled into the bush as the
heavily armed wolfers and a few traders approached the
camp. Although some of the Assiniboine made threatening gestures, others talked to Farwell who had come into
the camp to try to defuse the situation. The effort failed. A
shot was fired and a massacre was under way. The wolfers
fired repeatedly into the camp with Henry and Winchester
repeaters. The Indians, who also had been drinking, were
apparently too drunk to defend themselves, and those few
who were able to fight only had muzzle-loading muskets.
Approximately twenty Indians were killed. The head of a
man who was beaten to death was severed from his body
and fastened to a tipi pole near the post.

Although none of the wolfers and traders was injured in
the vicinity of the camp, one was killed as he pursued
survivors. Five Assiniboine women were captured, the
tipis and their belongings were burned, and the five
women raped during the drunken orgy that followed the
massacre. Before the wolfers and traders left the next day,
they set the posts on fire.

Reconstructed, the Farwell post is part of a national
historic park.

30 ROCHE PERCEE—In 1857 members of the Palliser expedition made a side-trip to the banks of the Souris River. The object of their attention was an unusual outcropping of eroded rock south-east of present-day Estevan. Although several rocks were pierced with holes, the one called Roche Percée was particularly impressive because of its prominence, size, and large hole. Palliser noted in his report that it was covered with petroglyphs and that 'the Indians never pass this stone without making some offering to the Manito...such as rubbing vermilion on it, or depositing beads, tobacco, or the like in the crevices.' The rock is still known as Roche Percée, but it has changed drastically. Shattered by lightning, the top of the 'hole' has collapsed. The distinctive feature of this well-known landmark no longer exists, and the petroglyphs have eroded away.

In 1873 the men surveying the international boundary camped near Roche Percée. The following year, on 24 July, the straggling column of officers and men belonging to the newly formed North-West Mounted Police arrived at the site. Discovering that members of the U.S. Cavalry and the Boundary Commission surveyors had carved their names on the rock, many of the policemen added their signatures, too.

The formation of the police force was one of a number of steps being taken by the Canadian government to prepare the North-West for settlement. On 23 May 1873, before the Cypress Hills Massacre, the bill establishing the North-West Mounted Police was given royal assent. News of the tragedy hastened the organization of the force.

The first recruits were sent to Lower Fort Garry, north of Winnipeg, for training late in 1873; three other troops joined them at Dufferin the following June. Then on 8 July 1874, 275 officers and enlisted men began their trek west to stop the illegal whisky trade and bring Canadian law and order to the North-West.

FORT WALSH, CYPRESS HILLS—A short distance north of where the Cypress Hills Massacre took place, Fort Walsh was built by the North-West Mounted Police in 1875. According to Cecil Denny, an officer who was on the trek west, the Cypress Hills region

was infested by whisky traders. It was a favourite hunting ground for many Indian tribes, and they were continually coming into conflict. Horse stealing was rife. Briefly, it was about as lawless a section as could be found in the territory.

Ridding the area of the illicit liquor trade and appealing to the Indian population to abide by the white man's laws were the immediate tasks confronting the detachment under the able leadership of Supt. James Morrow Walsh. Two new crises, however, were looming on the horizon. By the end of 1876 several thousand Lakota Sioux were seeking safety in the Wood Mountain region east of the Cypress Hills following their defeat of Custer at Little Bighorn in

Montana. To further complicate matters, hunger had become a reality on the northern plains, and a growing number of Canadian Indians were forced to move into the Cypress Hills to hunt.

To cope with the potentially dangerous proximity of large camps of traditional enemies, Fort Walsh was named headquarters of the force. The detachment was enlarged and three outposts were established, including one at Wood Mountain. A bustling village soon developed several hundred metres north of Fort Walsh, to serve the police, Métis hunters, freighters, and Indians who used the fort as a rendezvous and stopping-off place. By 1881 Fort Walsh's usefulness had come to an end. The Lakota had been persuaded to return to American territory, and the Canadian Indians had been escorted out of the Cypress Hills towards reserves located some distance from the border. The post was dismantled and the site abandoned. Today Fort Walsh is a national historic park.

32 SOUTH OF WOOD MOUNTAIN—Chief Sitting Bull and some of his people camped in the clay hills along Short Creek, south of Wood Mountain, during the winter of 1876–77. Other Lakota Sioux continued directly to Wood Mountain. Sitting Bull joined them in the spring, his band swelling their numbers to nearly 5,000.

Walsh made contact with the various groups of Lakota as they arrived. He explained the conditions that would have to be met if they intended to stay on Canadian soil, and later reported: 'My opinion is they will obey the law of the country. War they appear to have had enough of.' The officer arranged for Jean Louis Légaré, the trader at the Métis settlement at Wood Mountain, to supply ammunition for hunting buffalo, which fortunately were in the area that winter.

A police post was established at Wood Mountain, and travel between it and Fort Walsh became frequent. The trip was trying for officers and men relatively inexperienced in frontier living, particularly during the winter. One officer described some of the difficulties encountered:

This part of the country... in the winter season [was] an undulating bare plain for a distance of one hundred and twenty miles, covered with snow, devoid of timber or wood of any kind, streams frozen to the bottom and no shelter but what the broken banks of a Coolee [sic] could afford... Wood had to be carried to melt the snow and heat water for tea. Most sparingly was this wood handled and when the little fire was made, the poor half-frozen party would gather around it to catch the smallest radiated spout of heat to try and warm their shivering bodies.

The local name for the land formations shown here is 'dobies', derived from 'adobe hills'. The area is now part of the Grasslands National Park.

OFFICE, WOOD MOUNTAIN NORTH-WEST MOUNTED POLICE POST—The Wood Mountain post was the focus of police activity during the four-and-a-half years that the 5,000 Lakota Sioux led by Sitting Bull were in Canada. Although buffalo were available the first winter, the next years were to be ones of increasing hardship. The herds vanished, and hunger stalked Indian camps across the North-West. The Canadian government informed the Lakota that American Indians were not entitled to rations. Accordingly, they would have to surrender to American authorities or starve. Yet the police could not ignore their pitiful condition. Left-over food at the tables was carefully saved and distributed as far as it would go among the women and children. Walsh, in April 1880, reported:

I was forced to make small issues of food to save their lives...
The conduct of those starving and destitute people, their patient

endurance, their sympathy, and the extent to which they assisted each other, their strict observance of law and order, would reflect credit upon the most civilized community.

Repeated efforts were made by both Canadian and American officials to get Sitting Bull and his people to return to their own country. Finally the suffering was too great. The Lakota gradually returned to the United States where, for the most part, they surrendered at American military forts and were assigned to reserves. Jean Louis Légaré, the respected and compassionate French trader who fed many of the Indians during the difficult times, was personally responsible for persuading Sitting Bull and a large group of his followers to travel south; he undertook at his own expense to supply food for the entire journey to Fort Buford. The post at Wood Mountain remained in operation to serve settlers until 1918; it has been partially reconstructed as a provincial historic park.

BUFFALO SKULL—The final disappearance of the buffalo brought to the North-West starvation, destitution, and death. The Cypress Hills were the last stronghold of buffalo in Saskatchewan. Indian bands from the Qu'Appelle Valley, under the leadership of such chiefs as Piapot and Cowessess, had been hunting in the region for a number of years. By 1877, Big Bear, Little Pine, and other chiefs from the Saskatchewan district were forced to move into the hills in their increasingly futile quest for buffalo. For all practical purposes the animal was non-existent in Canada by the end of 1879, so the Canadian buffalo hunters moved even farther south, into the United States, to hunt. Within two or three years the American buffalo were also extinct, and the bands of Cree, Saulteaux, Assiniboine, and Dakota Sioux straggled back to Fort Walsh. Supt. L. N. F. Crozier, who had replaced Walsh as officer in charge of Fort Walsh, reported that

the Indians commenced coming in large numbers from [American territory]... where they had wintered. In every instance they were starving. Many said they had but little to eat during the greater part of the winter... Men and teams were kept constantly on the roads with provisions to meet and feed the starving camps as they arrived. The number of Indians increased daily, until at one time there were as many as 5000 about the Fort.

Disease was rampant as whooping cough, measles, diarrhea, dysentery, and scarlatina swept through the Indian camps. Many died, with the children being hit the hardest. The government wanted the Indians to stay away from the American border, so plans were made to close the fort. Accompanied by a detachment of police and a supply of provisions, chiefs and their followers were escorted east and north to begin a new life. An era of independence and freedom had ended. Ironically, the buffalo bones that remained behind became the first 'harvest' hauled by the new Canadian Pacific Railway; thousands of tons of bones were transported to eastern markets where they were ground into fertilizer.

FORT BATTLEFORD—Developments along the North Saskatchewan River during the 1870s differed considerably from those in the Cypress Hills region. Here the emphasis was on settlement. The North-West had become part of Canada in 1870 and was given the name 'North-West Territories'. Two years later the route for a transcontinental railway through the parkland region was examined by a team of specialists, and plans to erect a telegraph line along the proposed route were initiated. In 1875 a base camp for the telegraph crew was set up near where the Battle River flows into the North Saskatchewan River, in what is now west-central Saskatchewan. The site, located on the south side of the Battle, became known as Telegraph Flat.

The Canadian government's decision in 1876 to estab-

lish the capital of the new North-West Territories near the junction of these two rivers set into motion a number of events. Several government buildings and a North-West Mounted Police post were constructed. The Hudson's Bay Company built a store, other businesses were established, and settlers came, creating the community of Battleford.

The police post was constructed under the supervision of Supt. James Walker on a plateau between the two rivers, while the government buildings, telegraph office, and most commercial ventures were located on the south side of the Battle River on or near Telegraph Flat. However, the flat was susceptible to flooding and the town site was later surveyed on the plateau. Fort Battleford is now a national historic park.

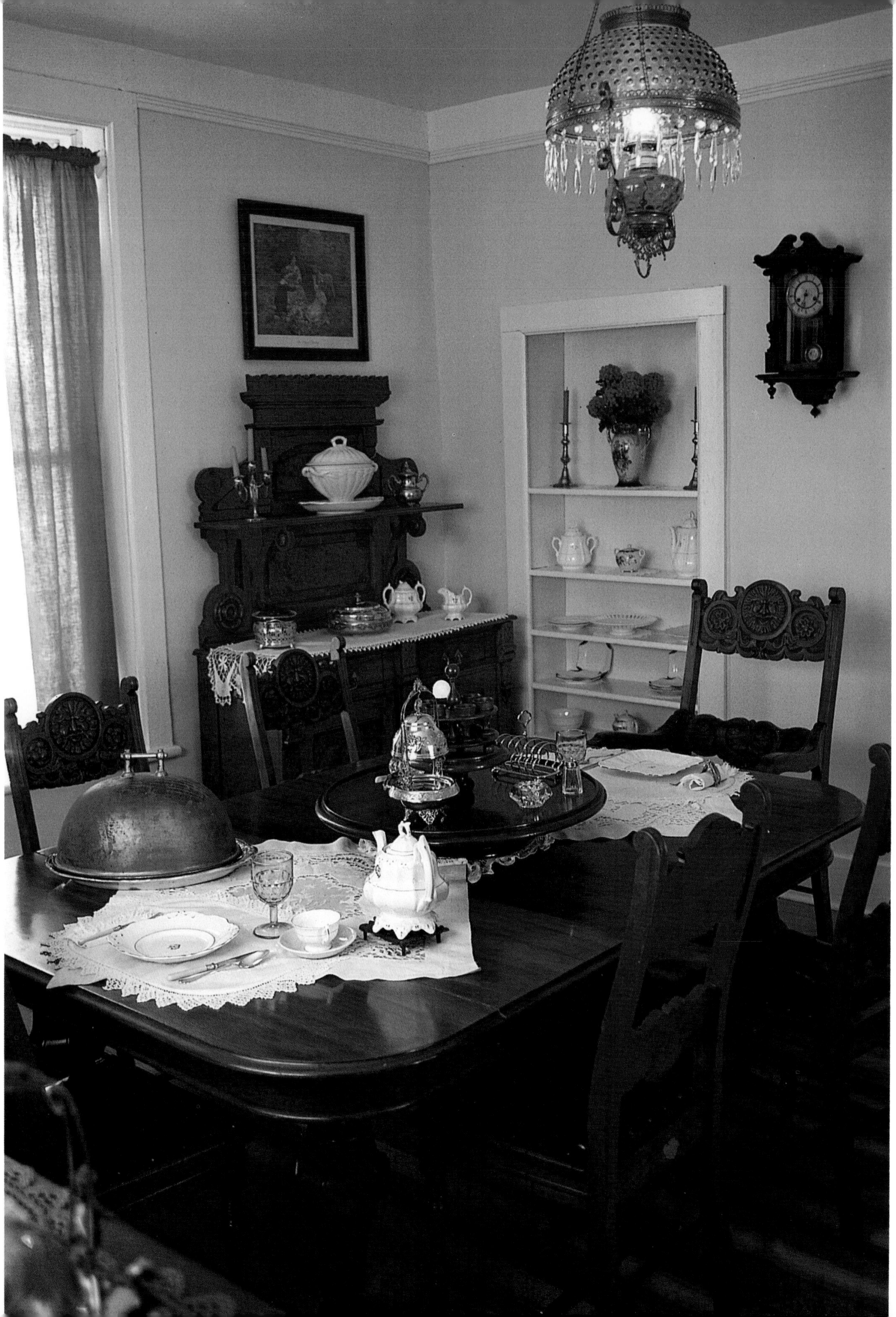

LIEUTENANT-GOVERNOR'S RESIDENCE, BATTLE-FORD

—The two-storey building constructed to house the lieutenant-governor of the Northwest Territories had a commanding view of the plateau where the police post was located. Made from logs, the building was covered with clapboard and the inside walls were plastered. According to the Department of Public Works' annual report for 1877, the 'accommodation' included a large reception room, a dining-room, and a drawing-room 'so arranged with large folding doors between that when...required they form one large room'. The building also contained a small office, large entrance hall, hat and cloak room, kitchen, summer kitchen, pantry, and eight bedrooms.

Although construction of the building was started in June 1876, it was not fully completed when Lieut.-Gov. David Laird and his family moved into the residence more than a year later. The North-West Council met there for the first time in 1878.

As capital of the North-West Territories, Battleford appeared to have a bright future. Homesteaders, merchants, and townspeople were drawn to the area by the promise of a railway. Steamboats navigating the Saskatchewan River delivered supplies and passengers, and in 1878 the Saskatchewan *Herald*, the first newspaper in the North-West Territories, began publication.

The optimism that accompanied the establishment of Battleford was dashed in 1881 when the decision was made to build the railway across the southern plains. A location on Wascana Creek known as Pile of Bones, later renamed Regina, was pin-pointed as the new capital; in 1883 the seat of government was officially transferred to the southern community that had developed by the creek.

The lieutenant-governor's residence was converted to religious and educational purposes. Declared provincial heritage property in 1984, it now stands empty.

COMMANDING OFFICER'S HOUSE, FORT BATTLE-FORD *(left)*

—Although the dining-room in the commanding officer's house at Fort Battleford has been refurbished using some of Supt. and Mrs. Walker's furniture and china, the house was not in fact as comfortable as it now appears. In a report dated 19 December 1879, Walker noted that his house and the barracks were in an unfinished state and were 'very uncomfortable':

We are now burning from four to five cords of wood per day, and it is only by keeping on fires night and day that the buildings are made habitable. This morning, with the thermometer 37° [F] below zero [–38°C], water was frozen on the top of the stove in my bedroom, notwithstanding there was sufficient fire in the stove to start the morning fire... There have been many cases of cold and rheumatism since the winter set in, caused, I have no doubt, by the cold winds blowing through the cracks in the buildings and the unusual fires that have to be kept up in the room to keep them warm.

FORT BATTLEFORD AT SUNRISE—In 1876 Treaty 6 was signed with the Cree, Assiniboine, and Saulteaux nations of the northern plains and parklands at Fort Carlton and Fort Pitt. Supt. Walker and part of his detachment from Fort Battleford served as an escort to the commissioners during treaty negotiations. Treaties with the Indians of the southern plains had already been signed, while inhabitants of the Cumberland House region signed an adhesion to Treaty 5 in 1876. The far northern Indians made treaty much later.

Although some bands moved onto reserves rather quickly after they signed treaty, a great many continued to hunt buffalo and follow their traditional way of life. When the buffalo disappeared, however, they had no choice but to settle permanently on their reserves and begin a new life based on agriculture. Patrolling the reserves and assisting with the distribution of annual treaty payments were among the police force's responsibilities.

Unfortunately, crops were poor, for both white and non- white farmers, during the early 1880s. The Indian people on reserves in the Battleford Agency, like Indians elsewhere in the North-West Territories, were living under dreadful conditions. Game animals were scarce, drought had wiped out crops, the government had drastically reduced rations in an effort to save money, and treaty promises had not been kept. Families were destitute, poorly clothed, and starving.

During the winter of 1883–84, Big Bear and other leading chiefs made plans to organize a united front for dealing with the government. The main concerns were improved living conditions and better treaty terms. The first meeting, scheduled for Poundmaker's reserve in June, was cancelled following a confrontation during a Thirst Dance with a farm instructor and the police detachment from Battleford. (The Thirst Dance is a religious ceremony sometimes referred to as the Sun Dance.) The chiefs of the Fort Carlton area met with Big Bear and Lucky Man later that summer. During a presentation of grievances to an Indian agent, Big Bear charged that the treaties they had signed were changed in Ottawa, with 'half the sweet things...taken out and lots of sour things left in'.

HOLY TRINITY ANGLICAN CHURCH, STANLEY MISSION (right)—Stanley Mission, which stands on the north shore of the Churchill River, is the oldest building in Saskatchewan and one of the most remarkable. It was built between 1854 and 1860 by the Rev. Robert Hunt for the Anglican Church Missionary Society. Of Gothic design, which in itself is unusual for the period and location, Holy Trinity was a magnificent building compared with the humble one-room structures the early missionaries and first settlers usually built.

The objectives of the missionaries who moved into the North-West during the mid-1800s centred on converting the Indian people to Christianity, while at the same time encouraging the development of small agricultural communities and the teaching of English moral and social values. In practical terms this meant persuading the Indians to give up their nomadic life of hunting and trapping, as well as their traditional religion, customs, and values.

When Hunt and his wife arrived in the La Ronge district in 1850, they were taking over missionary work begun in 1845 and 1846 by two native catechists. Hunt was an ordained minister from England. He considered several locations before choosing this particular site for the new mission in July 1851. Overwhelmed by the task before him, he wrote in his journal:

My Parish is certainly a large one, about 600 miles by 400 miles, with authority from the Bishop... to preach the Gospel 'in the regions beyond', but what I have seen of the country while coming hither forces the conviction upon me that there are few spots in this district that I can visit for this purpose. All is either forest through which none but an Indian can find his way, or naked rock, or swamp, or lake or river; without a solitary pathway through any part of it, except those ones made by the voyageurs at the portages.

The site where the mission is located was initially called Church Mission Point; the name was later changed to Stanley Mission in honour of Mrs. Hunt's home in England.

HOLY TRINITY ANGLICAN CHURCH, STANLEY MISSION—Hunt brought with him on the boat from England stained glass, window frames, hinges, locks, and other essentials for building an impressive church. Some of the original glass is still contained in the large sanctuary window shown here. In total, more than a thousand pieces were used in this and thirty-seven smaller windows. It is believed that Hunt also brought a sundial with him for installation in the top section of the steeple.

Before Hunt started work on Holy Trinity Church, he attended to other priorities, including the construction of a mission house, school, carpenter's shop, warehouse, store-room, cow house, and ice house. It took six years of hard work, from 1854 to 1860, for Hunt to complete his church. He was assisted by local Indians, several carpenters, and men from the Hudson's Bay post that was established in 1853 across the river from the mission. An Anglican bishop who visited Hunt before the building was complete reported that Holy Trinity would have made an 'admirable cathedral church' if it had been made from a material other than wood.

A small community developed at the mission. As the years passed, however, the population gradually shifted to the south bank where community facilities were being developed near the Hudson's Bay complex. Of the changes made to the church since 1860, the shortening of the spire has been the most dramatic. The church is still used, but title was transferred to the province of Saskatchewan in 1981. The church was designated provincial heritage property, and extensive repairs have been carried out. Holy Trinity is now part of Lac La Ronge Provincial Park.

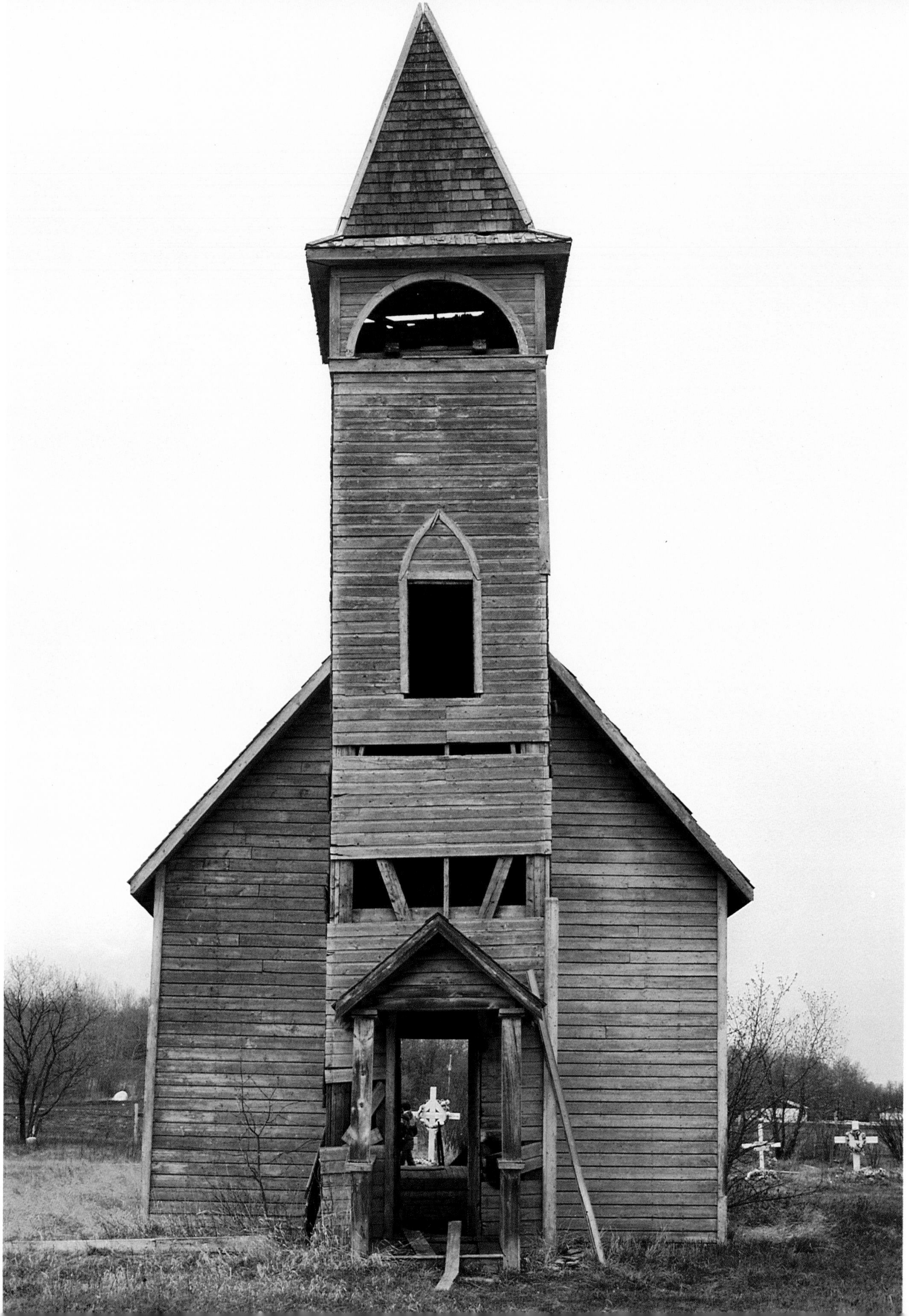

NISBET PRESBYTERIAN CHURCH AND SCHOOL, PRINCE ALBERT—The Rev. James Nisbet arrived at Fort Carlton with his family and several others on 17 June 1866 to establish a mission for the Presbyterian Church in the vicinity of the North Saskatchewan River. The officer in charge of Fort Carlton discouraged the location of a mission near his post, and after some consideration Nisbet decided to settle eighty kilometres downstream near a small community known as the Isbister settlement.

Nisbet was pleased with the site chosen for his mission, writing, 'The more that I see of the place where we have pitched our camp, the more am I satisfied of the excellence of the locality for a settlement.' He called his mission Prince Albert, in honour of Queen Victoria's consort. The Hudson's Bay Company established Fort Albert near the Isbister-Nisbet settlement later the same year. The community attracted settlers and flourished, gradually pushing Fort Carlton into obscurity.

The small log church and school, erected by Nisbet his first year in Prince Albert, was moved to its present site in Bryant Park in 1932.

ST. BARNABAS ANGLICAN MISSION, ONION LAKE —Weathered by the passage of time and abandoned after a new church was erected, St. Barnabas recalls memories of the first missions established on Indian reserves in the new North-West Territories. Chief Seekaskootch (Cut Arm) had selected a reserve at Onion Lake for his band of Woods Cree after signing Treaty 6 in 1876. The reserve, north of the North Saskatchewan River and adjacent to the present-day Saskatchewan–Alberta border, was surveyed three years later. The Rev. Charles Quinney founded St. Barnabas mission on the reserve around 1883 for the Anglican Church Mission Society. During the early days of the 1885 uprising, Seekaskootch helped Quinney and the Indian agent and their families escape to Fort Pitt, the Hudson's Bay post a short distance south of Onion Lake.

In 1892, when John Matheson arrived at Onion Lake to take charge of St. Barnabas as catechist and teacher, he found the church leaning at an angle and had it buttressed. The building was moved to a new foundation just north of its original location in 1904 and largely rebuilt.

44 MISSION ST. FLORENT, QU'APPELLE VALLEY—In 1865 Archbishop Taché planted a cross on a hill overlooking the Qu'Appelle Valley to mark the general location of a mission to be built by the Oblates of Mary Immaculate, a religious order of the Roman Catholic Church. Called St. Florent, this was one of the earliest missions established by the Catholic Church in what is now southern Saskatchewan. Today Stations of the Cross lead to a small chapel overlooking Mission Lake, and a large Catholic church stands by its shore.

Eleven years earlier Taché, as a young priest, had been instrumental in founding St. John the Baptist Mission at Ile-à-la-Crosse, the first Catholic establishment in the province.

St. Florent was built by Father Ritchot in 1866, the year after Taché's visit. Tragedy struck three years later when the small log building with a thatched roof was destroyed by fire and a Mr. Desjarlais died while trying to save the vestments and vessels. A new church was blessed in 1871 and renamed Sacré Coeur de Jesus in 1884.

The mission was built to serve the Métis buffalo hunters who wintered in the shelter of the Qu'Appelle Valley and spent the summers on the vast plains beyond. There were also several permanent residents in the area, since a number of Métis worked for the Hudson's Bay Company at Fort Qu'Appelle and had homes nearby. The post occupied a site on the other side of the valley, at the opposite end of the lake. The community of permanent and semi-permanent residents grew after 1870 when Métis from the Red River Settlement moved into the region. As the buffalo disappeared from the plains and the Métis turned to farming, fishing, and freighting for their livelihood, the Qu'Appelle Valley became a centre of Métis settlement.

Fr. Decorby took charge of the mission in 1868 serving until he was replaced by Fr. Hugonard in 1883. When Hugonard was appointed principal of the Indian Industrial School adjacent to the mission in 1884, Fr. Lebret assumed duties as parish priest. The settlement that developed around the mission officially became known as Lebret when a post office was opened at the mission in 1885.

ST. LAURENT—The original buildings are gone, but a log church marks the site near the South Saskatchewan River where an early Roman Catholic mission and a Métis settlement once flourished.

The community evolved over a number of years. During the 1860s, Métis buffalo hunters wintered at camps along the South Saskatchewan River east of Fort Carlton. One of these groups was led by Gabriel Dumont, a respected leader and noted buffalo hunter. By the fall of 1870, a large number of Métis, dissatisfied with life in the Red River Settlement, had moved into the area and built log cabins at a number of winter camps. In response to a request for a priest to minister to their spiritual needs, Fr. Moulin was sent from Ile-à-la-Crosse. Fr. André replaced him the following spring, spent the summer on the plains with the buffalo hunters, and returned with them to 'the wintering place'. There he established the St. Laurent Mission. Nearly fifty families built homes near the mission, while another 200 families located elsewhere along the South Saskatchewan.

Métis from the various camps held a meeting in December 1871 to discuss the establishment of a permanent settlement. According to Lawrence Clarke, the officer in charge of Fort Carlton, it was

resolved by all present that in the interests of themselves and families, it was necessary that they should abandon their wandering habits, and fix themselves at or near Carlton, as a permanent colony... This Colony once started will rapidly become strong and influential. The founders are far from being poor men, they are rich in horses and have all, more or less money at their disposal.

In a census taken by Clarke, the Métis population living adjacent to the mission consisted of forty-four men, fifty-eight women, thirty-nine children over twelve, and 159 children under twelve. Clarke noted that not one hunter made less than £100 sterling from 1 June to the end of December, and many had cleared between £200 and £500. He added that there were 577 horses in the community.

A new site was selected for the permanent settlement. St. Laurent de Grandin was officially established in the summer of 1873, and a provisional government was formed in December with Dumont as president. A log church was erected in 1874, a dormitory and residential school in 1875, and a convent in 1883.

ST. ANTOINE DE PADOUE CHURCH AND RECTORY, BATOCHE—In the early 1870s, Xavier Letendre, more commonly known as Batoche, opened a store and built a ferry where the Carlton Trail crossed the South Saskatchewan River. A small Métis settlement and commercial centre soon developed on the east bank. Facilities included several stores, a 'stopping place', and a blacksmith shop, all operated by local Métis. Oblate priests founded the Parish of Batoche in 1881, and two years later the construction of St. Antoine de Padoue Church and its rectory was undertaken.

Although many of the Métis continued to hunt buffalo for as long as the animals were available, others became increasingly involved in freighting, commercial ventures, and small-scale agriculture on narrow lots fronting the river. However, like White settlers in the Prince Albert area and elsewhere in the Saskatchewan River valley, the Métis were hampered by drought and poor crops, economic depression, and lack of political representation. Their plight was further aggravated by problems getting legal title to the land they had occupied since the 1870s.

Government indifference to western grievances and concerns frustrated and angered all sectors of the population. Protest meetings were held in Prince Albert, and a variety of groups sent petitions to Ottawa, but without success. In June 1884 a delegation travelled to Montana to ask Louis Riel, who had successfully championed the Métis in Manitoba, to lead the struggle for Métis rights and the redressing of settlers' grievances in the Prince Albert area. Riel made Batoche his base. As the Métis leader became increasingly militant and his religious views more pronounced, the priests and most of the English-speaking half-breeds and White settlers withdrew their support from the protest movement.

MASS METIS GRAVE, BATOCHE—The grave of Métis killed during the uprising of 1885 is a stark reminder of the tragedy that shattered the communities of the South Saskatchewan River region. Enclosed by a square of pickets, the grave is now part of a national historic park.

On 19 March 1885 Riel proclaimed a provisional government at Batoche with Gabriel Dumont as 'Adjutant General of the Métis nation'. The telegraph line was cut, hostages taken, stores seized, and an ultimatum issued for the surrender of Fort Carlton. A chain of irrevocable events had been set in motion. The first shots were fired near Duck Lake on 26 March when North-West Mounted Police from Fort Carlton, strengthened by volunteers from Prince Albert, skirmished with Dumont's Métis and were defeated.

It was determined that Fort Carlton could not be de-fended, and the post was abandoned in flames as the police and volunteers retreated to Prince Albert. Dumont and his men returned to Batoche. Before long the Métis received word that Maj.-Gen. Frederick Middleton and several militia units were marching from Fort Qu'Appelle towards Batoche. Riel had stopped the fighting at Duck Lake, declaring enough blood had already been shed. Now he discouraged Dumont from embarking on a campaign to harass Middleton's troops. In an oral account given in 1889, Dumont said he pointed out to Riel that the enemy was being given

too many advantages... Convinced that it was wrong to let him [Middleton] move about as he wished, I notified Riel that I could no longer follow his humanitarian counsels and that I had decided to go and fire on the invaders and that my men backed me up in this.

FISH CREEK, SOUTH OF BATOCHE—Dumont set up an ambush for Middleton and his field force at Fish Creek on 24 April. Although Dumont's men were hidden in a treed coulee, the general's scouts detected tracks and other signs of their presence. The element of surprise was lost. Dumont's fighting force of 150 men was quickly reduced to fifty-four as inexperienced fighters fled from the militia's artillery. Nevertheless, a handful of concealed Métis marksmen successfully forced Middleton's 400 men to retreat after a sustained battle. Middleton set up camp near Fish Creek, while Dumont's group went back to Batoche, their departure apparently unnoticed by the militia.

A large number of Middleton's men were volunteers, rather than 'regulars', and the fighting had been difficult for them. One of the senior officers later wrote:

None of us are ever likely to forget the dark night of the 24th close to the deep ravine, still holding for all we knew, a concealed enemy, and with us nothing but raw troops, totally unaccustomed to night work, and hampered by wounded men... We thought we had come out for a picnic, and it was impossible to help feeling that a war's hardships are doubly cruel to the civilian soldier.

Middleton had been surprised by the fighting ability of the Métis, and it was to be two weeks before he continued his march. The next encounter, at Batoche, took place 9–12 May. Fighting from well-prepared rifle pits and breast-work of earth, rock, and logs, the Métis withstood militia charges for three days. Finally, reduced to firing gravel, nails, and tacks from muzzle-loaders, their lines broke. The Métis were defeated.

Riel surrendered to Middleton on 15 May. He was tried for treason in July, pronounced guilty, and hung in Regina on 16 November 1885. Dumont evaded capture and left for the United States several days after the defeat. Thirty-eight Métis were charged with treason-felony. Nineteen were released on their own recognizance, eighteen sentenced to prison, and one acquitted. Six of seven Indians charged with treason-felony, along with the Métis, were sent to prison.

Two White men associated with Riel were also charged with treason-felony. One was acquitted, and the other found not guilty due to insanity. Many of the Métis and Indians were given early pardons in 1886 and released from the penitentiary. Dumont returned to Canada in 1888 after a general amnesty was granted. The Métis who died were buried in a mass grave at Batoche.

Fish Creek is now a national historic site.

INTERPRETIVE SIGNS, FRENCHMAN'S BUTTE—At Red Deer Creek, slightly north of Frenchman's Butte, Maj.-Gen. T. B. Strange and his Alberta Field Force exchanged shots with Plains and Woods Cree who were under the leadership of Wandering Spirit and Ayimisīs. This occurred on 28 May 1885 in one of the most indecisive skirmishes during the tragedy of 1885.

Wandering Spriit and Ayimisīs, who were part of Big Bear's Plains Cree camp, had initiated the killing of nine White and half-breed men on 2 April at Frog Lake (located in present-day Alberta north-west of Lloydminster). Big Bear had tried to stop the bloodshed, but he was too late. The war chiefs took over the leadership of the camp, ending Big Bear's peaceful, ten-year struggle to obtain better conditions for his people.

On 13 April a large group from Big Bear's camp, augmented by Woods Cree from the district, travelled southeast to the Hudson's Bay Company's Fort Pitt. The following day they demanded the surrender of the post. The police stationed at the fort were allowed to escape unharmed, and the Hudson's Bay employees, their families, and others in the post were given a choice of leaving with the detachment or surrendering to the Indians. The civilians all chose to surrender. After looting the store at Fort Pitt, the Plains and Woods Cree returned to Frog Lake with forty-four prisoners and wagons full of food, clothing, and other supplies. Most of the prisoners were put in the care of the Woods Cree, who were resisting plans to join Riel and Dumont at Batoche.

Fort Pitt was plundered again in May, only this time several buildings were set on fire as the group left to hold a Thirst Dance at Frenchman's Butte. By now the Indian camp consisted of approximately 300 men, 700 women and children, prisoners, horses, and dogs. From a number of Indian accounts it seems that a considerable number of Woods Cree had joined Big Bear's camp for protection, since they did not know what the police would do when they arrived.

They were soon to find out. On 25 May, government forces led by Strange arrived at the still-smouldering ruins of Fort Pitt. According to W. J. McLean, the officer in charge of Fort Pitt and a prisoner in the Indian camp, the Indians abandoned the Thirst Dance and moved to the north bank of Red Deer Creek, where

many of the women and a few of the men were busy digging pits [with sharp flat pointed sticks, tin pans, etc.] which they covered over with round logs of greenwood, and in which they took shelter that night.

The men, in the meantime, were throwing up earthworks,

sighting their rifles, and testing for 'the range from bank to bank of the valley of the creek'.

Aided by heavy fog, some of the Woods Cree and their prisoners managed to slip away from the camp. The prisoners were released several days later. Before Strange's force attacked the main camp on the morning of the 28th, the women, children, old men, and remaining prisoners were taken to a safe spot some distance away. The fighting lasted a number of hours. The gunner manning Strange's cannon finally found his range, and the ammunition-poor Indians withdrew. Strange, in the meantime, decided it was too risky to cross the creek under fire and withdrew in the opposite direction. Thus ended the 'battle of Frenchman's Butte'. Frenchman's Butte, located north-east of Lloydminster, is now a national historic site.

STEELE NARROWS—The final shots of 1885 were fired at a narrows at Makwa (Loon) Lake many kilometres north of Fort Pitt on 3 June. After leaving Frenchman's Butte, the Plains and Woods Cree and twenty-four prisoners fled north through mosquito-infested marsh, woodlands, and swamps. The group, which included more women and children than men, travelled in heavy rain, waded through waist-deep swollen creeks, and slept in wet clothes. Food was scarce, and both prisoners and Indians suffered.

The large group reached the ford between Makwa Lake and Sanderson Bay on 2 June. Fort Pitt's McLean, with his wife and nine children, were among the prisoners. He later described what happened at the narrows:

The most of the Indians crossed the ford in the afternoon and we had to cross also. The Woods Crees crossed the younger members of my family on horse back, but the older ones had to wade, with my repeated assistance. The ford was over four feet deep. We camped on a fine arm of the lake about a mile and a half beyond the ford. Several of the Indians did not cross the ford that evening, and the next morning [June 3] they were surprised and attacked by Major Steele and his scouts, about eighty strong [probably closer to fifty], and four of them were shot before they crossed the ford.

One of the Woods Cree shot by the scouts was Seekaskootch, the chief who during the early days of the 1885 uprising had helped the Indian agent, the Anglican missionary, and their families escape from Onion Lake after the killings at Frog Lake. The chief had also played a significant role in protecting the prisoners during their stay in the Indian camp.

When the Indians on the far side of the ford heard the firing, they rushed to help their companions crossing the narrows. In a skirmish that lasted about half an hour, Steele's scouts were unable to cross the ford under fire, and since a flanking movement was impossible, the officer ordered a return to the base camp. Middleton and his forces, accompanied by the scouts, arrived at the narrows four days later. The general crossed one ford and then decided the muskeg was impassable for his transport and artillery. The chase was abandoned, and the entire column returned to Fort Pitt. In the meantime, the Woods Cree and their prisoners deserted the Plains Cree and headed north-west. On 18 June, McLean and the other captives were released and started the 225-kilometre trip back to Fort Pitt.

The ford was officially named Steele Narrows in 1962.

52 CUT KNIFE HILL, POUNDMAKER RESERVE—Chief Poundmaker lies buried beneath a framework of tipi poles on Cut Knife Hill. It was here, on 2 May 1885, that Poundmaker's band successfully defended their camp against an attack led by Lieut.-Col. W. D. Otter.

The events that precipitated the assault had begun more than a month earlier. In late March, Plains Cree and Assiniboine from reserves in the Battleford Agency travelled to Battleford to present their grievances to the Indian agent and to receive details on the fighting that had occurred between the police and Métis at Duck Lake. When word of the Indians' approach reached Battleford, homes and businesses were abandoned as residents fled to the protection of the police post. The agent would neither meet with the delegation nor issue rations. Angry and frustrated, the Indians started looting homes and stores. Most of the group returned to their reserves the next day or else joined Poundmaker's camp at Cut Knife Creek. In isolated incidents two Assiniboine men killed a local farmer and an Indian department farm instructor, and several buildings in the town of Battleford were burned.

Meanwhile, 200 men and 300 women and children remained barricaded for three weeks within the police stockades waiting for an attack that never came.

Otter arrived with his troops from Swift Current on 24 April. On his own initiative and without proper authority, the officer decided to take 'part of [his] force at once to punish Poundmaker'. Accordingly, on the afternoon of 1 May, 325 men with forty-eight supply wagons, a Gatling gun, and two dilapidated seven-pounder field guns left Battleford. Otter arrived at Cut Knife Hill early the following morning and took up a position on top of the hill. The Cree and Assiniboine mobilized quickly. After a fight that lasted some seven hours, the government troops were almost surrounded. When Otter ordered a retreat, Poundmaker prevented his own men from pursuing the withdrawing force. Otter was later to note that 'had they done so, much delay and loss of life might have been entailed upon us, as the country was favourable to them'.

Cut Knife Hill and Poundmaker's grave have been designated heritage property by the Poundmaker band, and the Cut Knife battlefield is a national historic site.

MASS GRAVE OF CONVICTED INDIANS, BATTLE-FORD—Poundmaker's band, and the others allied to him, moved towards Batoche to join Riel following the defence of the camp at Cut Knife Hill. But the Indians were too late to be of any assistance. The Métis were defeated on 12 May, before the group arrived. Fourteen days later, Poundmaker surrendered to Middleton at Battleford.

Some of the Woods Cree surrendered at Fort Pitt following the battle at Frenchman's Butte on 28 May. Most of the Woods and Plains Cree who had fled north turned themselves in within a month of the engagement at Steele Narrows. Ayimisīs, Lucky Man, and Little Poplar were among those who escaped to the United States. Wandering Spirit, whose black hair turned grey in less than two months during that tragic summer, gave himself up at Fort Pitt. Big Bear successfully evaded three columns of troops and surrendered to a small detachment of North-West Mounted Police near Fort Carlton; ironically, this was one of the few militia units not searching for him.

In the trials that followed, Wandering Spirit and ten other Indians were convicted of murder without benefit of legal counsel and sentenced to die. Three were later reprieved. The remaining eight, including Wandering Spirit, were hanged at Battleford and buried in a mass grave on the bank of the North Saskatchewan River near the North-West Mounted Police fort.

Poundmaker and Big Bear were both found guilty of treason-felony at trials in Regina and sentenced to three years in the penitentiary. Poundmaker was released the following year, but died within a few weeks. Big Bear, found guilty with a recommendation for mercy, was detained longer and not released until 1887 when prison officials feared he would die in prison. Since Big Bear's band had been dispersed during his confinement, the old chief had neither a band nor a reserve. He died early in 1888 on Poundmaker's Reserve. Another fifteen Indians were convicted of treason-felony, sent to prison, and eventually pardoned.

PRAIRIE ELEVATORS—As the rails of steel crossed the southern plains, stakes driven into the virgin prairie sod marked the location of future railway stations and grain elevators. By 1883 a string of villages had sprung up almost overnight near the station sites. Newly arrived settlers unloaded their belongings at places such as Moosomin, Qu'Appelle, Regina, and Moose Jaw, and then hauled their freight by cart and wagon to their homesteads. Eventually branch lines and other railways extended into distant parts of the Territories, opening up millions of acres for development.

Settlers sometimes preceded stations and towns. When Mr. and Mrs. Seward T. St. John and their party travelled by train from Nebraska in 1902 to homestead south-east of Moose Jaw, freight cars carrying their household belongings, equipment, and livestock were dropped off at a railway siding at Milestone. Mrs. St. John wrote in her diary on 9 April:

On orders from the Superintendent at Moose Jaw (Mr. Milestone), our cars were placed on the rear of a freight train and moved twelve miles northwest to our location, marked only by milepost 35. There is no siding, spikes are drawn, the rails in turn are swung to one side, and our cars are pushed out on to the prairie, where they will remain until a siding is built. Thus began the town of Wilcox [named in honour of 'Bert' Wilcox, a CPR official at Moose Jaw].

The surveyors arrived ten days later to lay out the town site. Lumber was shipped by train and hauled by wagon to the St. John's homestead three kilometres from the Wilcox siding. On 2 May the couple moved into a 3.6-by-4.5-metre shack on their new farm.

OLD LOG BUILDINGS—Shelter from snow, wind, and rain has always been a priority for people living in the northern plains and parklands region. For the pioneer settlers, their first homes varied, depending on where they staked their claim, how much money they had, and how far they were from the railway. Often the first shelter was a 'dugout', which was made by digging a cellar and roofing it with poles, sod, and hay.

In wooded areas, log houses were built as the first permanent homes. These were often small and cramped, and when a larger home was built, the original became a chicken coop, a barn, or a place to store grain.

OLD LOG BUILDING EXTERIOR—When properly built, log houses were warm in the winter. Construction methods varied, but caulking between the logs with moss or a similar material was crucial for a draft-free structure. To provide extra protection, particularly if the logs were of poor quality or did not fit together snugly, the house was 'mudded' or plastered. This usually consisted of mixing clay with a fibrous material like straw. The mixture was plastered over willows or strips of wood that were fastened to the wall as lathing. The straw helped hold the clay together after it dried, while the willows provided extra anchorage. The mud was put on thick enough to cover the lathing completely, and then the surface was smoothed over. When the wall dried, it was whitewashed, if lime could be found nearby. Rain, the hot sun, and intense cold all deteriorated the coating; mudding the houses thus became one of the jobs that had to be done each fall in preparation for winter.

INTERIOR OF SOD HOUSE AT ELBOW—Homesteaders moving to the southern plains usually found that timber for logs was non-existent. They made their homes from the only natural building material available: long strips of sod plowed from virgin ground. Because windows, hinges, and lumber for the floor and framing were the only costs involved in building a sod house, it was only slightly more expensive than erecting a log building.

Sod houses were warm in the winter and cool in the summer, but notorious for leaking roofs. So much so, it was said, that if it rained outside for one day it rained inside for two. The thick draft-free walls were made by stacking strips of sod, grass side down, like bricks. It was not unusual for the walls to be about one metre thick at the base, tapering slightly as they were built upward. Space was left for a door and windows, while the infamous roof was made from boards or poplar poles covered with hay and a layer of sod. Although the furniture was simple, the women made curtains and added other decorative touches to make a comfortable home.

Some homesteaders, such as Mr. and Mrs. Seward T. St. John, settled near a railway and were able to get lumber to build a shack covered with tar paper as their first home. From Mrs. St. John's description, contained in her diary entry for 7 December 1902, the shack was not particularly comfortable:

A blizzard rages all day... In the evening put paper on the inside of the shack, which is constructed of only one thickness of shiplap lumber; if it keeps on, it will soon be all cracks. With the stove and bed there is so little room left, we hang the chairs on spikes driven into the beams.

Even her new frame house, completed the following year, was not weather-proof, and she discovered once during the worst blizzard of the 1903–04 winter that 'snow was drifted half way across the room.'

MALTBY HOUSE, CANNINGTON MANOR—Not everyone who travelled to the hinterlands of Canada wanted to be a farmer. Edward Pierce, the founder of Cannington Manor, was one of these men. He and his upper-middle-class family immigrated to western Canada from Great Britain in 1882 after running into financial difficulties. Pierce chose land on the edge of Moose Mountain in present-day south-eastern Saskatchewan for his new home, close to where a number of people from eastern Canada, England, and other parts of the British Empire had already settled.

The Pierces spent the first winter in the earth cellar of their partially finished house. Unaccustomed to cooking, housework, and the isolation of the plains, the first winter was particularly hard on Mrs. Pierce and her daughters. For the men there were long hours of hauling both firewood and building logs a distance of sixteen kilometres, because 'there was none on the plain and the slow-going oxen made a day's trip of it.'

After his arrival at Cannington Manor, Pierce promoted the immigration of other British families, particularly those with some financial backing, to his settlement. Yet Pierce's personal ambitions extended beyond farming. In a letter to Ottawa, he wrote,

It is the universal desire, as soon as the districts are incorporated, that I shall represent the people at Ottawa... There is a pile of work to be done here of which I am more fitted to undertake, than grubbing up the land around me for grain growing etc.

In 1884 Pierce formed a partnership and established the Moose Mountain Trading Company. Ernest Maltby, the man who lived in the house pictured here, joined the partnership in 1886 and also served as the local postmaster. By 1892, when he married, the original log house had been enlarged by adding two wings, and the outside was covered with clapboard siding. Maltby also built a tennis court beside his house.

Cannington Manor has been partially rebuilt and is now a provincial historic park.

ALL SAINTS ANGLICAN CHURCH, CANNINGTON
MANOR—Although Edward Pierce donated land for All
Saints Anglican Church and was a prime mover in its
founding, the construction of the building was a community affair. Logs were hauled from nearby Moose Mountain, and in June 1884 a church-raising 'bee' was held.
Sufficient funds were solicited in England to pay local
carpenters to finish the interior and to buy a second-hand
organ. The church, fully paid for by June 1885, was the
first consecrated Anglican church in the Diocese of
Qu'Appelle.

The establishment of a church during the formative
years of a settlement was common to many communities
that developed in the North-West Territories. Nevertheless, Cannington Manor could not be considered a typical
frontier village. In an attempt to transplant the social
customs and activities of upper-middle-class Victorian life
to the tiny village on the prairies, Pierce and the others
who joined him adopted the stance that just 'because you
have come into the wilds it is not necessary to forget
civilization'. Thus in the Pierce home, according to one of

his daughters, breakfast and lunch were eaten in the
kitchen, but 'the supper tradition must be adhered to—
clean [table] cloths, polished silver, flowers when possible,
changed frocks, discarded overalls and a shutting off of all
farm duties.' On the social scene, fox hunts, horse racing,
formal afternoon teas, and elaborate dances characterized
the settlement.

For all practical purposes Cannington Manor had become a company town by 1889 with the Moose Mountain
Trading Company owning most of the buildings in the
village and operating the majority of the businesses. But
the years were not good ones for the homesteaders or the
business men. Frost and drought destroyed crops, wheat
prices were low, and the entire North-West was in a
depression. The community lost its aggressive leader when
Pierce died in 1888. When it was learned that the railway
was being routed sixteen kilometres south of Cannington
Manor, many of the English settlers gave up their dreams
of a Victorian oasis in the midst of the Canadian prairie
and moved elsewhere. By 1900 the village had been abandoned.

NORTH-WEST MOUNTED POLICE MESS HALL, RE-GINA—Transformation from a wet canteen, dispensing what was probably the cheapest beer in town, to a chapel is part of this building's history. Now known as the RCMP Chapel, the building is located on the grounds of the Royal Canadian Mounted Police Depot Division and is considered to be the only free-standing, police-owned chapel in the world. It is designated a municipal heritage property and has the distinction of being the oldest building in Regina.

After Regina was named the new capital of the North-West Territories in 1882, the decision was made to transfer the North West Mounted Police headquarters from Fort Walsh to Regina. The barracks were laid out near Wascana Creek some three kilometres west of the railway station and the collection of tents, shacks, and newly constructed frame-houses that formed the nucleus of the new capital.

The first buildings at the police barracks were portable ones transported in sections by rail from eastern Canada. The following year, in 1883, a contractor was hired to erect the building shown in this picture. It originally served as a mess hall and had a kitchen annex on the west

side. A canteen for 'supplying comforts to the men' sold items such as shoe-laces, tobacco, and toothpaste. A few years later the 'comforts' were expanded to include draft beer, which was sold in pewter mugs for five cents a pint. In Regina the price was fifteen cents. The establishment of the 'wet' canteen was based on experiments conducted by the U.S. Cavalry to control the drinking habits of its men. It was also an extension of the policy to provide recreation rooms at the barracks, a step recommended by Commissioner A. G. Irvine who had reported in 1882 that

too much amusement during relaxation cannot be provided for the men in this country, where there is so little of any kind obtainable, in the winter especially. Amusement will be had, and if not provided will be sought, and many evil effects will result.

A fire in the spring of 1895, which presumably started in the kitchen, resulted in the closing of the building. On the suggestion of Mrs. L. W. Herchmer, wife of the commissioner who replaced Irvine in 1886, the mess was converted to a chapel. The mess and wet canteen were moved to another building. The chapel was consecrated on 18 December 1895.

62 STONE SCHOOLHOUSE, SASKATOON—The first settlers in the Saskatoon district responded to advertising by the Temperance Colonization Society, which promoted 'prosperity, peace, and plenty' in a land 'free from the accursed influence of the liquor traffic'. Their destination in 1883 was 86,265 hectares of land straddling the South Saskatchewan River that had been granted to the Society by the Canadian government. The settlers became known as the Temperance Colonists, and the site chosen for the colony's administrative centre by John Lake, on behalf of the society, was called Saskatoon.

One early homesteader recalled that when they arrived in Saskatoon the morning of 3 June 1883, 'the only building was a sod house, about twelve by twenty.' It was located across the river from the future site of the Bessborough Hotel, a contemporary landmark in Saskatoon. During the first year, the settlement was a collection of tents, shacks, and sod houses. Most of the colonists, of course, moved onto homesteads instead of living in the village, and they occupied similar dwellings. In 1884 the government inspector of colonization companies reported:

Saskatoon townsite is a pleasant one and there are erected on it several handsome and substantial buildings—school house, hotel, stores, private residences, etc., while a good ferry is provided for crossing the river. The settlers are of an excellent class . . . The total number of settlers is 80.

A woman who arrived that same year was less impressed, saying 'they called it the City of Saskatoon, but when we arrived there were seven houses, and not one properly finished.'

Two years later four stone buildings erected by Alex Marr gave the settlement a hint of stability and permanence. The little stone schoolhouse was built in 1887. It was the focus of social and educational activity during the early years of settlement and remained in use until replaced by a new two-room school in 1902. A few years later the stone school was dismantled and reconstructed on the grounds of the new University of Saskatchewan to make room for a larger school on the original site. The stone schoolhouse, which has been restored as a school museum, is considered the oldest public building in Saskatoon.

MARR RESIDENCE, SASKATOON—During the uprising of 1885, the Marr residence served as a field hospital for wounded militiamen. It is one of the few buildings from that early period to survive and today has the distinction of being the oldest building in Saskatoon still on its original location.

The first of the wounded arrived in the city on 1 May following the skirmish at Fish Creek. Dep. Surg.-Gen. T. G. Roddick, a leading surgeon from Montréal, wrote in his diary on 7 May that he had

requisitioned the three largest houses in the place for hospitals, so as to concentrate the wounded, and thus lighten the work of attendance... There are about twenty wooden dwellings and a commodious schoolhouse in the place... The buildings referred to, which I requisitioned, were especially well placed on the bank of the river, and, being unfinished, could be conveniently arranged for hospital purposes.

On 14 May the *Northcote* steamboat delivered the wounded from Batoche. Many of the Temperance Colony women volunteered to help cook, care for the sick, and do laundry. In addition all available eggs, butter, and flour were purchased from the settlers, and many of the men found employment of various kinds with the militia. So Saskatoon, like several other White settlements in the North-West Territories, benefited economically from the 1885 uprising.

The Marr house, originally 5.5 by 7.3 metres in size with an attached kitchen, was built in a style popular in eastern Canada during the 1870s and 1880s. Alex Marr was a stonemason and contractor. Although the family, which included Mr. and Mrs. Marr and six daughters, moved into the house in the fall of 1884, only the two rooms at the front of the building had been completed.

During this century, renovations have included an enclosed front porch and a two-storey addition on the back. The house was purchased by the city of Saskatoon in 1979 and is currently being restored as heritage property in co-operation with the Meewasin Valley Authority.

64 FIEGUTH HOMESTEAD, TIEFENGRUND—Until the 1880s most of the immigrants who came to the North-West Territories were of British origin. This gradually changed as newcomers from continental Europe were drawn by promises of cheap land and freedom from political and religious persecution, servitude, and hunger. After 1896 the trickle of non-British immigrants turned into a flood, and the North-West Territories became a land of cultural diversity.

Johann Fieguth, grandfather of the photographer whose work appears in this book, came to the Rosthern Mennonite Colony north of Saskatoon in 1896. Fieguth had immigrated from West Prussia to the United States in 1886 and had lived in Oregon for ten years before moving to Canada. He built the house shown here on his homestead near Tiefengrund, north-west of Rosthern. Made from logs, it was covered with siding at a later date. Photographer Menno Fieguth and his father Ernest were both born in this house.

Gerhard Ens, who arrived in the Rosthern area in 1892, was the first Mennonite to settle on a homestead in the area. For a time he operated a store and post office in a box car loaned by the CPR. He later became an immigration agent and was largely responsible for recruiting Mennonites to the area. Ens was elected to serve in Saskatchewan's first legislature in 1905.

German-speaking Protestant pacifists, the Mennonites were attracted to Canada by government promises of free land, educational and cultural autonomy, and exemption from military service. They fell into two general groups. Some, like those who moved to the Rosthern area, settled on individual homesteads. The conservative Mennonites lived in villages and followed a traditional and separatist lifestyle.

UKRAINIAN CHURCH, (right)—The first Ukrainians to settle in what is now Saskatchewan came reluctantly in May 1897. Many were almost penniless. They had immigrated under the impression that the Canadian government would give assistance in the form of sustenance grants, tools, and cattle, in addition to free land. When the group arrived in Winnipeg by train, along with hundreds of other Ukrainian immigrants, they learned that the steamboat agents had misled them. Angry, the large group refused to leave Immigration Hall until some form of assistance was assured.

Government officials, faced with the impending arrival of hundreds of new immigrants, called the police. The hall was evacuated, and attempts were made to load immigrants onto a train scheduled to leave for Yorkton the following morning. When the immigrants refused, officials made veiled threats and left the railcars on a siding. An immigration official later reported:

Only two or three families actually got on the cars that night... We found by the next morning that about twenty-one families had come back... and got into the cars for protection, and were willing to go to Yorkton. I might say that the rain fell in the night, and this also had a cooling effect upon those who were sleeping out.

Approximately nine newly arrived families also agreed to board the cars. This trainload of settlers, and the others who followed that summer, settled at Saltcoats, Crooked Lake, and Beaver Hills in the Yorkton area of what is now east-central Saskatchewan.

BETH ISRAEL SYNAGOGUE, EDENBRIDGE—In 1906 a hill in a heavily wooded area near Carrot River became the focal point for a Jewish community that was established north of Melfort in east-central Saskatchewan. The fifteen founding homesteaders were originally from Lithuania and other parts of Europe but had been living in South Africa for several years before immigrating to Canada. They called their new community Edenbridge.

One member of the group, Hirsch Wolfovitz, had been sent ahead to look for a suitable location. He visited Jewish colonies at Hirsch, Wapella, and Lipton—all located on the treeless prairie—and then headed north towards the Carrot River and land that was more like his homeland in Lithuania. The others joined him, travelling by train as far as Star City and then by horse and buggy for some twenty-one kilometres.

A cabin, which later became known as the Edenbridge Hotel, was constructed from poplar logs on the Wolfovitz homestead. The roof was made from small poplar poles laid across poplar joists and covered with sod and clay. A loft, reached by means of a ladder, served as sleeping quarters for the men. The women and children slept on the main floor. During the first summer most of the men selected homesteads and then obtained temporary work with road gangs to help with the expenses of building homes and acquiring farm implements and oxen. And like settlers elsewhere, until they could afford transportation, they walked.

Farming was a new and sometimes frustrating experience for members of the Jewish colony. A neighbour befriended the group and gave assistance when it was needed. A demonstration of the intricacies of ploughing straight furrows with an ox-drawn plough prompted one of the colonists to write in his diary, 'That was when we found out it was harder to be a farmer than a store clerk.'

Construction of the synagogue was undertaken in 1907. It was completed in 1909 and remained in use until 1964. The Beth Israel Synagogue is the oldest in the province and has been restored by the Jewish community as an historic site.

CARROT RIVER (left)—Homesteaders who farmed in the parkland had timber for building and for firewood, but the work involved in preparing the land for cultivation was increased many times over. Armed with axes and logging chains, they had to clear the land of trees and stumps before the ground could be ploughed. Many of the newcomers had no practical farming experience. Furthermore, some arrived with little in the way of material goods. It was a common practice for the men to settle their families as best they could and then leave the women and children alone while they searched for work on railway construction gangs or on more prosperous farms. The money they were able to save was used to buy flour, tools, implements, oxen, and other necessities for survival. For the women, it was a distressful time, marked by a tremendous amount of responsibility, loneliness, hardship, and tears.

DOUKHOBOR PRAYER HOME, VEREGIN—The fact that this prayer house is situated on land purchased by Peter V. Verigin on behalf of the Doukhobor community, not on land granted to the colony by the government of Canada, in itself tells part of the story of the settlement of this religious group in Saskatchewan.

In 1899 nearly 7,500 Doukhobor pacifists fled to Canada to escape persecution by the Russian government. The Canadian government agreed to exempt them from military service and to permit the establishment of communal villages on three reserved blocks of land. A total of fifty-seven villages were established. On the two reserves north of Yorkton, the colonists in the main adhered to a communal way of life. The Doukhobors who settled in the Saskatchewan Colony north-west of Saskatoon, near Rosthern, lived in villages, but they tended to farm independently.

Within three years the government was putting pressure on the Doukhobors to register for homesteads as individuals, although Clifford Sifton, minister of the interior, assured them that 'those who will take their homesteads . . . may live together in one or more villages . . . [and work land near the village] instead of being compelled to cultivate each quarter-section held by each Doukhobor.'

Verigin, the Doukhobor leader, anticipated problems

with land holdings and in 1903 purchased twenty square kilometres of non-reserve land along the newly completed Canadian Northern Railway. He created a village, called it 'Verigin,' and moved his headquarters there. The town of Veregin, which grew from this settlement (the spelling not exactly the same as its founder's name), is north-east of Yorkton.

By 1907 the government had succeeded in breaking up the Doukhobor reserves by ruling that land must be owned and worked by individuals. Approximately a thousand independent-minded Doukhobor farmers agreed to sign for privately owned homestead land. The majority refused. In response the government drastically reduced the size of the reserves, and more than half of the Doukhobor lands were opened up to the general public. Verigin bought land in British Columbia, and 5,000 Saskatchewan Doukhobors relocated there with him.

The two-storey prayer home shown here was built in the Veregin village in 1917–18 by colonists who remained in Saskatchewan. Living quarters were located on the second floor. The main floor was used for meetings and religious services. The Prayer Home was declared provincial historic property in 1982 and is now part of the National Doukhobor Heritage Village.

ST. JOHN'S MINSTER CHURCH, LLOYDMINSTER—

Early in 1903 nearly 2,000 British men, women, and children answered the Rev. Isaac Barr's challenge to immigrate to Canada. Travelling together, they set out for a tract of land in the vicinity of the North Saskatchewan River near the present-day Saskatchewan–Alberta border. Although the group took individual homesteads and did not live in communal villages, the settlement was known as the Barr Colony, and they as the Barr Colonists.

Barr's association with the group was short-lived. Accused of mismanagement and profiteering, he was deposed as self-proclaimed leader before the group reached the land reserved for them. He was replaced by the Rev. George Exton Lloyd, an Anglican minister who accompanied the group as chaplain.

A log church was built by the colonists in 1904 at the town site that developed into Lloydminster, named after the chaplain ('minster' means a large or important church). The church became the centre of social and religious activity during the first days of settlement.

Oliver Holtby, one of the original colonists, described Christmas festivities held in the church in 1904:

Never was [there] a better Christmas party than the 2nd winter... It was the first to be held in the new log church, built of logs from ONION LAKE [north of the settlement], subscribed for by the people, logs squared by the ONION LAKE people, and freighted down...

Supper was provided by the women. Entertainment included a concert, and Santa Claus distributed presents to everyone, including the 'Mountie and other public men'.

Although the Barr Colonists were relatively well-off, bringing an average of £250 to £300 with them, many of the men and older boys looked for work after arriving in the North-West. Still, they had problems. With few exceptions, the colonists had no experience farming or handling wagons and livestock, and many apparently were not aware of what homesteading actually involved. Holtby wrote that his father soon left for Toronto to find 'more suitable' work, before long sending for his wife and daughters to join him.

The colony's church, St. John's Minster, has been moved from its original location to Weaver Park and is preserved as an historic site.

QU'APPELLE VALLEY—During the last quarter of the nineteenth century, with the buffalo gone and settlers moving into the North-West Territories, the life of the Indian people living on the plains and in the parklands underwent rapid change. Under the terms of treaties signed at Fort Qu'Appelle in 1874 and Forts Carlton and Pitt in 1876, the chiefs selected traditional land for their reserves. A number, including Piapot and Cowessess, eventually chose land along the Qu'Appelle Valley.

The Indian people soon found that their lives were heavily regulated by the Indian agents and farm instructors placed on their reserves. Permission was needed to leave a reserve, and often rations were given only in exchange for work, even when crops failed. When crops were good and there was a surplus, the Indians were nevertheless prohibited from freely selling them off the reserve.

In the early 1880s the Canadian government introduced the concept of Indian industrial schools. These schools were owned by the government but operated by the churches. The first one was established at Battleford in 1883 and was under the supervision of the Anglican Church. The following year a similar school was opened in the Qu'Appelle Valley adjacent to the Roman Catholic mission at Lebret. It was operated by Oblate priests and the Grey Nuns Community of Sisters. A third school, sponsored by the Presbyterian Church, was built in Regina in 1891.

The purpose of the industrial schools was to convert children to Christianity, 'civilize' them, and teach them

the skills required for coping in a changing world. In theory this meant teaching religion, reading, writing, and arithmetic, in addition to domestic, trade, and agricultural skills. In practice it meant taking the children away from their parents, imposing Christianity on them, attempting to eradicate traditional Indian values and beliefs, and providing training for only the most menial occupations. Hair was cut—including braids, which were an inherent part of being Indian. Children were punished when they spoke their own languages, and Indian names were replaced with Anglo-Saxon ones. The industrial schools were eventually replaced by boarding schools operated by various church denominations. Many of these schools are now owned and controlled by Indians.

OLD SCHOOL, CUMBERLAND HOUSE (left)—While newcomers were building a new life in a new land, the Indians, half-breeds, and Métis were adapting to the changes taking place in their homeland. In an area such as Cumberland House, where a living could still be made from trapping and fishing, the adjustments were not as drastic as in the southern regions where the traditional way of life had been destroyed.

The community at Cumberland House had developed around a fur-trade post built on Pine Island on the Saskatchewan River delta. The Anglican Church Missionary Society established a mission and school in the Cumberland-The Pas region during the 1840s; local residents were exposed to Christian teachings for a good many years before an adhesion to Treaty 5 was signed in 1876. In his report, the treaty commissioner noted that the Indian bands in the area were in 'a position to receive at once from

the Government the grant allowed for the maintenance of schools of instruction... They desired that the assistance promised should be given as soon as possible.' Although construction of the government-assisted school was initiated in 1881 on the reserve laid out near Cumberland House, it was not completed until 1907. In the meantime, the Anglican Church operated a school, intermittently, on the reserve.

During the 1870s, Métis from the Red River district moved to Cumberland House and the Catholic Church established a mission in the settlement. Fr. Charlebois, with the assistance of local Indians and Métis, built the small log school pictured above in 1890 and furnished it with home-made equipment. The Cumberland House Public School District was organized in 1892, and in 1905 a local school tax was levied.

W. R. MOTHERWELL HOMESTEAD, NEAR ABERNETHY

W. R. Motherwell was one of the first settlers to homestead in the Abernethy district north-east of Regina. Twenty-two years old and a recent graduate of the Ontario Agricultural College, he left Ontario in the spring of 1882, travelling by train to the end of the steel near Brandon and then by wagon to an area north of the Qu'Appelle Valley. He spent the first winter in a tent, built a log house in 1883, and then spent the next fourteen years developing a prosperous farm.

A co-founder of the Territorial Grain Growers' Association, Motherwell was elected the association's first president in 1902. The initial objective of this organization was to combat grain delivery problems that had developed with the railway and elevator companies. Motherwell served as Saskatchewan's first minister of agriculture from 1905 to 1918 and was federal minister of agriculture in the 1920s. During his career as a farmer and public official, he promoted the development of improved grain varieties and dry-land farming practices.

'I took a vow to myself,' Motherwell once said, 'that if I ever got in position where I could do it, I would try to reverse the idea that farming is a subservient occupation.' That thought may have been foremost in Motherwell's mind as he carefully collected field stones, one by one, from prairie coulees over a number of years. In 1897 those hand-picked stones were used to build the stately house that became a show-piece for the area.

The front section of the house originally contained a dining-room, formal and informal parlours, an office, and family bedrooms. The smaller section at the back included the kitchen, a summer kitchen, and bedrooms for the hired help. Landscaped with flower beds, ornamental trees, and shelter-belt plantings of trees, the farmstead featured a tennis court and dugout that provided the farm's water supply.

Three years after the death of his first wife in 1903, Motherwell married Catherine Gillespie. A Presbyterian missionary and principal of the File Hills Indian Residential School, Mrs. Motherwell was an advocate of women's rights and was active in women's organizations such as the Saskatchewan Homemakers Club. In one report she declared that women were losing respect and consideration because they had gradually sunk 'into the position of toy and slave, forced to assume a slavish attitude toward... [their] lord and master'.

The Motherwell homestead has been restored as a national historic park.

THE BECKTON HOUSE, NEAR CANNINGTON MANOR—For eight short years this stone house was the focus of an extravagant and somewhat unconventional way of life on the southern plains. The story began in the mid-1880s when nineteen-year-old Ernest Beckton and his eighteen-year-old brother William were sent from England to attend Edward Pierce's agricultural college for young British gentlemen at Cannington Manor. In 1887 Ernest and William inherited a large sum of money. With their younger brother Herbert they put money and efforts into what they hoped would become the best horse-breeding stable in western Canada. The Becktons called their venture 'The Didsbury Stock Farm'.

Horses, trainers, grooms, and jockeys were imported, and a magnificent stone barn lined with mahogany boards was erected. The Becktons' orange and black racing colours became known across western Canada and in the northern American states. The brothers also raised foxhounds and were avid participants in fox chases and other sporting activities popular with the upper-middle-class English folk who had been attracted to Cannington Manor.

The twenty-room stone house built by the Becktons was completed in 1889. It was lavishly furnished and decorated in a manner befitting wealthy young English gentlemen and became the social centre of the community, especially among the young bachelors. The house contained a 'bachelors' wing' (on the left side) for overnight guests. Phyllis Walsh, who was the granddaughter of Cannington Manor founder Edward Pierce and Ernest and Jessie Beckton's niece, stayed at Didsbury many times as a youngster. She described the bachelors' wing as

probably the most comfortable and luxurious suite between Winnipeg and Vancouver, richly carpeted in warm reds, with guest quarters, card rooms and a writing room. Its main feature was a full sized billiard table in a long room complete with all accessories, a fireplace and deep leather arm chairs.

But the sporting life at Didsbury was to be short-lived. The Beckton brothers were not good business men, and the money soon started running out. William was the first to return to England. In 1897 the other brothers, with their families, also left, and Didsbury farm was abandoned.

BIG MUDDY BADLANDS—This wild and broken land of deeply cut ravines and eroded sandstone has meant different things to different peoples. For the Indians who once lived here, it was a place to pray and fast, a holy place. Boulders arranged in the outline of a turtle lie on top of a high hill overlooking Big Muddy Lake. Several kilometres to the west, another boulder effigy—this one of a buffalo—has taken form. For American cattle and horse thieves, natural caves in the rugged outcroppings became hide-outs. Stories of outlaw gangs terrorizing the region became part of the history of the ranchers who settled in the area.

The badlands flank Big Muddy Creek and Big Muddy Lake north of the United States border between Estevan

and Wood Mountain. By the 1880s the North-West Mounted Police were making regular patrols of the area to stop whisky smuggling from the United States, and several ranchers had started running herds along the Big Muddy.

At the turn of the century, authorities in Montana began cleaning up the frontier lawlessness in their state, and a number of cattle rustlers, horse thieves, and train robbers crossed the border. Using caves in the Big Muddy Badlands as their base, Dutch Henry's rustlers and the Nelson-Jones Gang worked both sides of the border, threatening ranchers, stealing livestock on one side, selling it on the other, and then stealing it again. The gangs joined forces in 1903 and became the legendary 'Wild Bunch'.

CATTLE NEAR MAPLE CREEK—The Maple Creek and Swift Current regions in the south-west corner of what is now Saskatchewan became centres of ranching activity during the 1880s and 1890s. In the Maple Creek area, Americans who drove cattle in from Nevada and Montana were among the first ranchers. Their ranks were joined by members of the North-West Mounted Police who remained in the Territories after completing their term with the force.

A number of large ranches were established by American and British entrepreneurs. These men took up the Canadian government's offer to lease up to 100,000 acres (42,500 hectares) of grazing land for a maximum of twenty-one years at an annual rent of one cent per acre. The 76, Turkey Track, and Matador ranches were among the greatest of the cattle empires in the Swift Current–Maple Creek areas.

These were the days of the open range, when cattle roamed unchecked by fences and farms. But as homestead-

ers pressured for land at the turn of the century, grazing leases were cancelled and restrictions were placed on ranching activities. Ranching was already in a vulnerable position when the disastrous winter of 1906–07 wiped out more than half the cattle population. Although the industry recovered, it never regained its former importance.

The attitude of many ranchers towards homesteaders is aptly illustrated by James Barnet Henson, a ranch hand who worked on the Matador. In his will, Henson directed his executors—among other things—to

sell by public auction the whole of my real estate . . . and with the monies thus procured to create a fund, to be ultimately used for the extermination of that class of Vermin, *commonly known as farmers, who are at present polluting by their presence, the country adjacent to the* South Saskatchewan River . . . *And finally I leave to each & every* Mossback *my perpetual curse as some reward to them for their labours is destroying the* Open Range *by means of that most pernicious of all implements, the plow.*

CANADIAN PACIFIC RAILWAY STATION, SASKA-
TOON—Railways helped shape the settlement of the Canadian North-West. Saskatoon is a prime example. When
the Temperance Colonization Society founded the tiny
community of Saskatoon in 1883, the town site was laid
out on the east bank of the South Saskatchewan River. The
railway was many kilometres to the south, and the community stagnated. In 1890, the Qu'Appelle, Long Lake,
and Saskatchewan Railway, *en route* to Prince Albert
from Regina, crossed the South Saskatchewan River at
Saskatoon. The line was leased to the Canadian Pacific
Railway. Ignoring the existing settlement, the CPR built its
station on the west side of the river. A new town was
immediately built in the vicinity of the station. It took over
the name Saskatoon, and the original settlement was renamed Nutana.

The villages continued to show little advancement until
1903 when 1,500 Barr Colonists arrived by train on their
way to establish Lloydminster. Saskatoon, with a population of some 400 people, was the closest railway point to
Lloydminster. For at least one colonist, Saskatoon was a
disappointment:

*We had expected to see quite a town... Instead we saw a few
houses and small stores on the east side of the railway track,
and a bunch of bell army tents on the west side... Even the
station was only a small shack.*

The colonists gave Saskatoon's economy a much-needed
boost. Before they left, money drafts for more than
$250,000 had been presented to the bank, and it was
estimated that nearly 1,000 head of horses, 500 wagons,

and 150 mowers and binders had been purchased. Some of
the Barr Colonists remained in Saskatoon, new homesteaders arrived, and by the fall of 1903 the population
had increased to 1,400. A new village, called Riversdale,
grew at the site where the colony's tent town had been.

In 1906 the communities of Saskatoon, Nutana, and
Riversdale amalgamated and were incorporated as the city
of Saskatoon. That same year the Canadian Northern
Railway took over the original railroad, crews moved into
the area to build two new lines (the Canadian Pacific and
the Grand Trunk Pacific) through Saskatoon, and in 1907
excavation for the new CPR station was undertaken. With
three railways passing through the community, Saskatoon's population more than doubled in three years. Construction boomed, and by 1912 the daily passenger trains
arriving or leaving numbered twenty-seven. The CPR
station built in 1907 is still in use.

THE BANK OF NOVA SCOTIA, MOOSE JAW (*right*)—
Moose Jaw was selected as a divisional point for the CPR
main line in 1882. For this community, and many other
'first' settlements along the railway, illegal bars and broth-
els were as much a part of the environment as railway
stations and hotels. According to a young American who
worked on the railway grading crew, in the twenty-three
days it took to grade the right of way between Moose Jaw
and Swift Current, Moose Jaw had grown from 'no tents
or anything' to

*quite a town. Lots of saloons and stores, and 20 side tracks all
built up... This town is mostly canvas tents brilliantly lit up
and everything in shape for the entertainment of strangers,
providing they have plenty of money.*

Local promoters started pressing for a brick factory as
early as 1884, but a kiln was not set up until 1890. As a
consequence, most early buildings were made of wood. In
1891 fire raced up the first block of Main Street, wiping
out more than seventeen businesses, destroying a church,
and claiming three lives. It was then made mandatory that
all buildings within a defined area had to be constructed
from brick or stone.

Like other larger Saskatchewan centres, Moose Jaw
boomed between 1910 and 1913. The red-brick building
trimmed with granite shown here was constructed by the
Bank of Montreal in 1911 and sold to the Bank of Nova
Scotia in 1922.

POST OFFICE, HUMBOLDT—The post office at Humboldt, constructed in 1911, is representative of the dignified Romanesque-type public building erected by the Canadian government during the early years of this century. Although it was called a post office, the building included a customs house, weights and measures office, inland revenue office, and an armoury. A shooting-gallery was located in the basement, and the attic contained five 'living' rooms. The Humboldt Post Office now serves as a museum and is a national historic site and municipal heritage property. Humboldt is located east of Saskatoon.

Unlike many Saskatchewan towns, Humboldt's history

precedes the construction of the railway. The name was first used for a telegraph office built in 1878 where the telegraph line crossed the Carlton Trail. After the CPR was built across the southern plains in 1882, a new overland trail developed that linked the town of Qu'Appelle, located on the rail line, with the Carlton Trail. A mail station was established at Humboldt, and overnight facilities were provided for stage coach passengers and other travellers. In 1886 the first 'highway' robbery in the North-West Territories took place south of Humboldt, creating a flurry of excitement.

BANK OF COMMERCE, WATSON (right)—The Bank of Commerce was often the first permanent, stable building to be erected in towns that developed along rail lines between 1905 and 1910. This was accomplished by manufacturing prefabricated buildings in eastern Canada and transporting them in sections by train. Soon after the track reached a town site, the components for a building were unloaded and then quickly erected using a patented sectional wall system.

The Bank of Commerce at Watson was erected in 1906 on the Canadian Northern trunk line that was built through central Saskatchewan. It is an excellent example of the largest and most pretentious of three types of prefabricated buildings erected by the Bank of Commerce in western Canada during this period. Designated municipal heritage property in 1982, the bank building in Watson has been a national historic site since 1977. Watson is 149 kilometres east of Saskatoon.

COURT HOUSE AND LAND TITLES OFFICE, SWIFT CURRENT—When the province of Saskatchewan was created in 1905, the provincial government took over the judicial system from the federal government. During the next few years a number of court-houses were built that reinforced the sense of law and order that had typified the settlement process. One of the most impressive was built at Swift Current in 1914, a year after the city had become headquarters of its own judicial district. It was the first of two court-houses in Saskatchewan that combined judicial facilities with a land titles office. The other one was built the same year at Humboldt.

During construction of these buildings it was pointed out that a 'Made in Canada' policy was being followed whenever possible and that 'all other things being equal preference is given to the Canadian material, and Canadian industries are being patronized.' The building is faced with Saskatchewan-made buff bricks and trimmed with Manitoba limestone.

Currently called the Court House, this building at Swift Current provides facilities for the provincial and Queen's Bench courts and the sheriff's office. It has been designated municipal heritage property.

NORTHERN CROWN BUILDING *(above)* AND C. W. SHERWOOD DEPARTMENT STORE, REGINA *(overleaf)*—In the space of a few years Regina progressed from a settlement much maligned because of its lack of trees, water, and natural beauty to a city of such magnitude that Wilhelm Cohnstaedt, a visiting German journalist, was prompted to write in 1909:

When you travel... to Regina... you will have the surprise of your life. Here, asphalt-paved streets lead you to an elegant hotel... You pass by an imposing City Hall that one would normally only expect in a big city and past a post office of sandstone and marble, which is the envy of one of my co-travellers from New York; there are large, almost over-elegant stores, and palatial banks, not to be outdone by the public buildings.

Some of the early buildings were particularly interesting. For example, a unique low-relief sculpture carved in sandstone was incorporated into the façade of the Northern Crown Building. The building was erected in 1905–06 for the Northern Bank. Operating out of Winnipeg, the Northern Bank was the first Canadian chartered bank to establish headquarters in western Canada. In later years it was absorbed by the Royal Bank.

Erected in 1913, after Cohnstaedt's visit, the Sherwood Department Store has been known as the Saskatchewan Wheat Pool Building for the past sixty years. The Gothic Revival styling of the brick-clad structure includes high-relief sculptures made from Atlantic terra cotta. The façade of this building has been designated municipal heritage property.

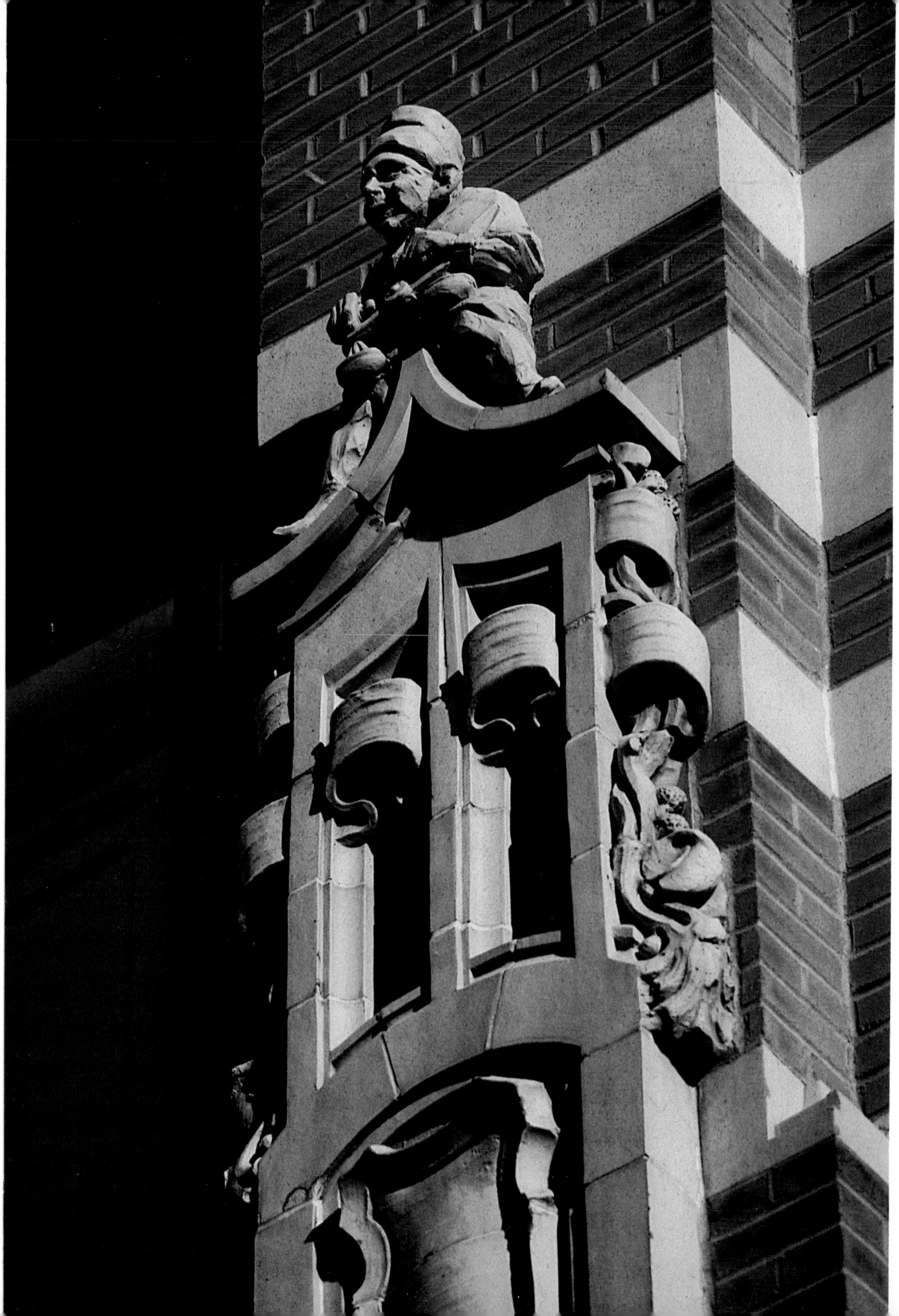

CANADA LIFE ASSURANCE COMPANY BUILDING, REGINA *(right)*—Better known as the Saskatchewan Government Insurance Office Building (SGIO), this structure was one of many erected in Regina immediately after a tornado cut a swath of destruction through the downtown and northern sections of the city on 30 June 1912. The storm destroyed some of the finest buildings in western Canada and reduced many homes, warehouses, and businesses to rubble. Three days later, on 3 July, the Regina *Morning Leader* reflected the optimism of the times: 'Nothing—mark the word nothing—can check Regina's progress... The new Regina... will far outrival the Regina that was so badly stricken last Sunday.'

The Canada Life Assurance Company Building is one of the best examples of the Chicago school of architecture in Saskatchewan. The marble and terra cotta medallions decorating the façade feature a pelican, the corporate symbol of the company. Designated provincial heritage property, the building has been restored by a private developer and given back its original name.

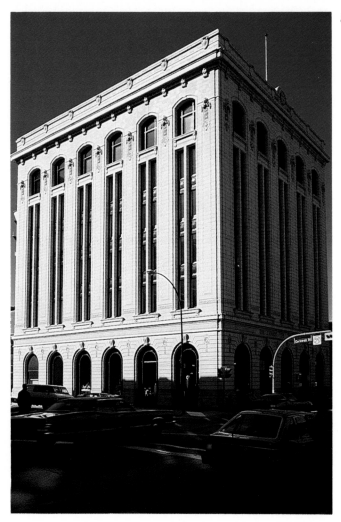

C. W. SHERWOOD DEPARTMENT STORE, REGINA *(left)*

COLLEGE BUILDING, UNIVERSITY OF SASKAT-CHEWAN, SASKATOON — The date was 7 April 1909, the event, one of the most exciting in the history of Saskatoon: the city had been selected as the site of the University of Saskatchewan. Whistles were blown and people crowded the streets when the news was received from Regina via telegraph at 11:30 p.m. The following day some 5,000 people gathered at Saskatoon's CNR station to welcome the men who had been instrumental in selecting the site.

Under the guidance of the university's first president, Walter Murray, the campus was designed and built 'not for a decade but for a century'. The College Building was to be the most important. Murray said the university must do 'something of interest architecturally... The building is the first one, and for many years will occupy the place of honour.'

It was built overlooking an open area of lawn and flower-beds that became known as 'The Bowl'. Constructed in the Collegiate Gothic style of architecture selected for the university, the building was faced with greystone taken from the banks of the South Saskatchewan River.

Currently called the Administration Building, it is a provincial heritage property.

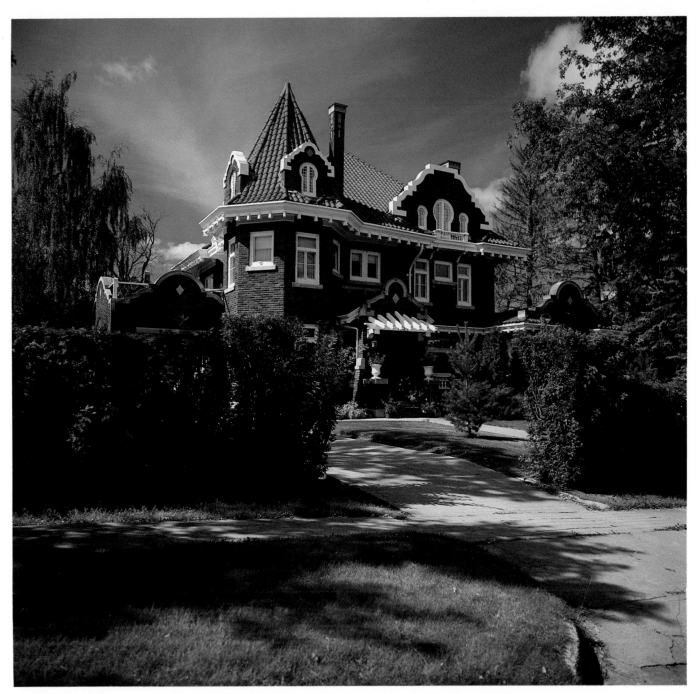

KEYHOLE CASTLE, PRINCE ALBERT—As construction and business activity in Saskatchewan's major cities climbed to a frenzied peak in 1912, signs of individual wealth became readily apparent. A two-and-a-half-storey brick residence in Prince Albert, nicknamed Keyhole Castle by local residents, was one of the most unusual. It was built by Sam McLeod, a Prince Albert business man, politician, and provincial magistrate who made his money in real estate and insurance.

Keyhole Castle was completed in 1913 at a cost of $42,000. Only the finest construction materials were used. The red roof tiles came from Cuba. The bathroom fixtures and marble for three fireplaces were shipped from Italy,

and the interior was finished with hardwoods imported from various parts of the world. Sterling-silver chandeliers hung from the living-room and dining-room ceilings, and an outstanding quality of stained glass was used in sliding doors separating these two rooms and in several windows. Even more unusual, a telephone intercom and a central vacuum cleaning system with outlets in each room were installed during construction.

The keyhole-shaped windows and the elaborately scrolled gable are rare in Canadian architecture. Still a private residence, Keyhole Castle has been designated a national historic site.

GOVERNMENT HOUSE, REGINA—In 1889 a residence for the lieutenant-governor of the North-West Territories was constructed to replace a portable building in use since 1882. According to Prime Minister John A. Macdonald, that building was 'a wretched place, and I do not see how the Governor's family live there during the winter... There were 17 stoves going continually, and the inmates could not keep themselves warm.'

The new residence was much more substantial. Nicholas Flood Davin, the first Member of Parliament for Assiniboia West and founder of the Regina *Leader*, described it as

a solid structure, and a structure that, while a handsome one, is not one that has any extravagance as to ornamentation. It is such a structure as a person representing the Government of Canada, and representing Her Majesty, and who is the head of society, as well as of political life in the North-west should have.

The residence was decorated and furnished in a proper manner for the Queen's representative. The ground floor included a drawing-room, dining-room, parlour, library, billiard room, kitchen, sewing room, servants' living quarters, dairy cooling room, wine vault, and brick safe. A staircase in the 'main' hall led to the fifteen bedrooms on the second floor.

Government House served as the lieutenant-governor's residence from 1891 to 1945. Designated provincial historic property, it has been restored to represent the turn-of-the-century period when it was the home of Lieut.-Gov. and Mrs. Amédée Forget.

LEGISLATIVE BUILDING, REGINA—Early photographs of this massive building being erected in the midst of a treeless plain lend credibility to the sincerity of the Regina *Leader* writer who stated that residents may 'justly regard [the legislative building] as a symbol of the magnitude and strength of the great Province of which they are citizens'.

Regina had almost always been a capital city. Its beginnings date back to 1882, when the spot where the Canadian Pacific Railway crossed Pile of Bones Creek was selected to replace Battleford as capital of the North-West Territories. The proposed town site was christened Regina on 23 August 1882, the day the first train arrived.

Some six weeks later, the Manitoba *Free Press* reported:

At present there are two tent stores in Regina, and some... railway camps, but as water has to be hauled from the creek three kilometres further west, the most of those desiring to do business at the new capital have camped up there, where there is no station. At the latter place there are two fairly stocked stores, two temperance saloons, and one large livery stable (all in tents), which appear to be doing a very fair business.

The North-West Mounted Police barracks, the first residence for the lieutenant-governor, and the Territorial Administration Building were built near the creek. Other government buildings were erected near the railway station located some three kilometres to the east. It was there, close to the station, that the main settlement of Regina developed.

The city was named capital of Saskatchewan after the province was created in 1905. The following year land on

the south side of man-made Wascana Lake was purchased for the new capital building, with construction getting under way in 1908.

Erected in the shape of a cross and topped with an octagonal dome, the legislative building was constructed in the Beaux-Arts architectural style. The building frame was made from reinforced concrete and faced with Tyndall stone from Manitoba. Although the building was not completed and officially opened until 1912, the 1911 session of the legislature met in the reading-room of the library. The legislative building, which is a provincial heritage property, is now the focus of a sixty-eight-hectare park containing government, university, cultural, and recreational components.

LEGISLATIVE BUILDING ROTUNDA, REGINA, AND AN OLD HOUSE, EAGLE HILLS *(right and overleaf)*—It is fitting that a mural on the second floor of the legislative building overlooking the rotunda pays tribute to the Indian people who lived on this land long before the arrival of the newcomers. The Cree, Assiniboine, Saulteaux, Sioux, and Dene helped European newcomers survive in this land. Later, men and women of mixed Indian-White ancestry—the English- and French-speaking half-breeds and the Métis—eased the transition from fur trade to settlement.

Although fur traders, politicians, surveyors, business men, railway builders, and eastern interests helped shape Saskatchewan, it was the pioneers from a multitude of countries and ethnic groups who actually settled the land,

populated it, and provided the labour that built the province. At first these newcomers came by the rivers. Then the railway was built, and settlement shifted from the rivers to wherever the twin lines of steel ran. The land was marked into squares and grids, the ground was ploughed, and trees were cleared.

Most of the homes built by the early settlers are not being preserved and eventually will disappear from the landscape, but the land they cultivated and the routes they followed will remain as lasting testimony to their efforts.

And elsewhere in the province, historic sites, buildings, and a variety of environments offer different points in the circle from which to view the uniqueness of historic Saskatchewan.

SOURCES FOR CAPTIONS

Materials from archival collections are listed in full. For more complete information on all other sources listed here, see the Bibliography, p. 93.

INTRODUCTION, p. v
Storm, *Seven Arrows*, p. 4.

PICTOGRAPHS, BETWEEN MARIBELLI AND HICKSON LAKES, NORTHERN SASKATCHEWAN, p. 3
Mackenzie, *Voyages From Montreal*, p. 83.

DRINKING FALLS, CHURCHILL RIVER, p. 4
Mackenzie, *Voyages From Montreal*, p. 83.

PORTAGE LA LOCHE, p. 5
Mackenzie, *Voyages From Montreal*, p. 90.

CLEARWATER RIVER, p. 7
Harmon, *A Journal of Voyages*, p. 137.

CREE LAKE, p. 8
Hearne, *A Journey From Prince of Wales Fort*, pp. 50-1.

THE SASKATCHEWAN RIVER, NEAR NIPAWIN, p. 9
M'Gillivray, *The Journal of Duncan M'Gillivray*, p. 18.

Henry, *Journal of Alexander Henry*, 28 & 29 August 1808.

POWDER HOUSE, CUMBERLAND HOUSE, p. 10
Hearne and Turnor, *Journals of Samuel Hearne and Philip Turnor*, p. 113.

RED RIVER CART WHEEL, FORT CARLTON, p. 12
McDougall, *Forest, Lake and Prairie*, p. 136.

REMAINS OF THE *NORTHCOTE*, CUMBERLAND HOUSE, p. 15
Church Missionary Society, Records and Correspondence, in Peel, *Steamboats on the Saskatchewan*, p. 28.

LAST MOUNTAIN HOUSE, p. 16
Cowie, *The Company of Adventurers*, p. 388.

OLD STORE AND POWDER HOUSE, FORT QU'APPELLE, p. 17
Cowie, *The Company of Adventurers*, pp. 212-13.

KATEPWA LAKE, QU'APPELLE VALLEY, p. 19
Harmon, *Sixteen Years in the Indian Country*, p. 76.

SOUTH SASKATCHEWAN RIVER VALLEY, p. 20
McDougall, *Pathfinding on Plains and Prairie*, pp. 94-5.

Cowie, *The Company of Adventurers*, p. 373.

Harmon, *Sixteen Years in the Indian Country*, pp. 72-3.

BULL'S FOREHEAD, p. 22
Chesterfield House Journal, 1801-02, B.34/a/3, fos.2d, 9, Hudson's Bay Company Archives, Provincial Archives of Manitoba.

GREAT SAND HILLS, p. 22
Macoun, *Sessional Papers*, No. 3, p. 17.

CYPRESS HILLS, p. 25
Hector, James, Saskatchewan Parks and Renewable Resources files.

Macoun, *Manitoba and the Great North West*, p. 252.

VIEW FROM BALD BUTTE, CYPRESS HILLS, p. 27
Cowie, *The Company of Adventurers*, pp. 303-4.

ROCHE PERCEE, p. 30
Spry, *The Papers of the Palliser Expedition, 1857-1860*, p. 130.

FORT WALSH, CYPRESS HILLS, p. 31
Denny, *The Law Marches West*, p. 76.

SOUTH OF WOOD MOUNTAIN, p. 32
Letter from unidentified North West Mounted Police officer to Cora Walsh, 21 May 1890, MG 29, C45, Public Archives of Canada.

OFFICE, WOOD MOUNTAIN NORTH WEST MOUNTED POLICE POST, p. 33
Report of Supt. J. M. Walsh, December 1880, in North-West Mounted Police, *Opening Up the West* (1880), p. 27.

BUFFALO SKULL, p. 34
Report of Supt. L. N. F. Crozier, December 1880, in North-West Mounted Police, *Opening Up the West* (1880), p. 30.

COMMANDING OFFICER'S HOUSE, FORT BATTLEFORD, p. 37
Report of Supt. James Walker, 19 December 1879, in North-West Mounted Police, *Opening Up the West* (1879), pp. 22, 24.

FORT BATTLEFORD AT SUNRISE, p. 38
Department of the Interior, RG10 file 15,423 (microfilm C10, 123), Public Archives of Canada.

HOLY TRINITY ANGLICAN CHURCH, STANLEY MISSION, p. 38
Robert Hunt in Saskatchewan Parks and Renewable Resources pamphlet, *Holy Trinity—Stanley Mission*, 1985.

NISBET PRESBYTERIAN CHURCH AND SCHOOL, PRINCE ALBERT, p. 43
'Letters of Rev. J. Nisbet, January 1867', published in *The Home and Foreign Record of the Canadian Presbyterian Church*, 1867, Biographies, James Nisbet, p. 14.

ST. LAURENT, p. 45
A letter from Lawrence Clarke to Donald A. Smith, 15 January 1872, Hardisty Papers, 154A.H264C, Glenbow-Alberta Institute Archives.

MASS METIS GRAVE, BATOCHE, p. 47
Stanley, 'Gabriel Dumont's Account of the North West Rebellion, 1885', pp. 258-9.

FISH CREEK, SOUTH OF BATOCHE, p. 48
Lord Melgrund in Morton, *The Last War Drum*, p. 68.

INTERPRETIVE SIGNS, FRENCHMAN'S BUTTE, p. 49
McLean, W. J., 'Reminiscences of the Tragic Events at Frog Lake and in Fort Pitt District With Some of the Experiences of the Writer and His Family During the North West Rebellion of 1885', p. 36, Copy No. 80, Hudson's Bay Company Archives.

STEELE NARROWS, p. 51
McLean, W. J., 'Reminiscences of the Tragic Events at Frog Lake and in Fort Pitt District With Some of the Experiences of the Writer and His Family During the North West Rebellion of 1885', p. 41, Copy No. 80, Hudson's Bay Company Archives.

CUT KNIFE HILL, POUNDMAKER RESERVE, p. 52
Lieut.-Col. W. D. Otter in Morton, *The Last War Drum*, p. 108.

PRAIRIE ELEVATORS, p. 55
St. John, 'Diary, March 30–December 25, 1902', p. 25.

INTERIOR OF SOD HOUSE AT ELBOW, p. 58
St. John, 'Diary, March 30–December 25, 1902', p. 28, and 'Diary, January 2, 1903 to March 30, 1904', p. 29.

MALTBY HOUSE, CANNINGTON MANOR, p. 59
Jessie (Pierce) Beckton, 'Cannington Manor, A Tale of Early Settlement Life', Special Collections, University of Saskatchewan Archives, p. 12.

Saskatchewan Parks and Renewable Resources pamphlet, *Cannington Manor*.

ALL SAINTS ANGLICAN CHURCH, CANNINGTON MANOR, p. 60
Jessie (Pierce) Beckton, 'Cannington Manor, A Tale of Early Settlement Life', Special Collections, University of Saskatchewan Archives, pp. 27–8.

NORTH-WEST MOUNTED POLICE MESS HALL, REGINA, p. 61
Turner, *The North-West Mounted Police, 1873–1893*, Vol. 1, p. 685.

STONE SCHOOLHOUSE, SASKATOON, p. 62
Mrs. Margaret Hunter in Saskatoon *Daily Star*, 24 November 1917.

Inspector's Report, 1884, Temperance Colonization Society, Dominion Lands Branch, Department of the Interior, RG 15, Vol. 653, File 174,266, Public Archives of Canada.

Mrs. Caswell in Kerr and Hanson, *Saskatoon: The First Half-Century*, p. 10.

MARR RESIDENCE, SASKATOON, p. 63
Dr. T. B. Roddick's Diary, 7 May 1885, in Klimko, *Preliminary Archaeological Investigations at the Marr Residence*.

ST. NICHOLAS UKRAINIAN CATHOLIC CHURCH, INSINGER, p. 64

W. F. McCreary, Commissioner of Immigration, in Kaye, *Early Ukrainian Settlements in Canada, 1895–1900*, p. 284.

BETH ISRAEL SYNAGOGUE, EDENBRIDGE, p. 67
Rosenberg, *Edenbridge: The Memory Lives On . . .*, p. 16.

DOUKHOBOR PRAYER HOME, VEREGIN, p. 68
Clifford Sifton in Tarasoff, *Plankun Trava: The Doukhobors*, p. 72.

ST. JOHN'S MINSTER CHURCH, LLOYDMINSTER, p. 69
Holtby, Oliver, 'Coming to Canada, 1903', C H742, Saskatchewan Archives Board.

OLD SCHOOL, CUMBERLAND HOUSE, p. 71
Thomas Howard, Commissioner, to Lieut.-Gov. Alexander Morris, 10 October 1876, in Morris, *The Treaties of Canada With the Indians*, p. 163.

W. R. MOTHERWELL HOMESTEAD, NEAR ABERNETHY, p. 72
Parks Canada pamphlet, *W. R. Motherwell Homestead*.

Motherwell, 'Women's Present-Day Responsibilities', p. 4.

THE BECKTON HOUSE, NEAR CANNINGTON MANOR, p. 73
Walsh, Phyllis Pierce, 'The Fragrant Wind', R-E1677, Saskatchewan Archives Board.

CATTLE NEAR MAPLE CREEK, p. 75
Photocopy of the Will of James Barnet Henson, of the ranch of The Matador Land & Cattle Co., 28 September 1919, and a Codicil, 9 May 1922.

CANADIAN PACIFIC RAILWAY STATION, SASKATOON, p. 76
Hordern, *Something Ventured—Something Gained*, p. 19.

THE BANK OF NOVA SCOTIA, MOOSE JAW, p. 76
Cyrus Bramble, from diary excerpts quoted in Knight, *All the Moose . . . All the Jaw*, p. 6.

COURT HOUSE AND LAND TITLES OFFICE, SWIFT CURRENT, p. 80
Government of Saskatchewan, *Public Service Monthly* (August 1914), p. 3, in Rostecki, *The Early Court Houses of Saskatchewan*, p. 89.

NORTHERN CROWN BUILDING AND C. W. SHERWOOD DEPARTMENT STORE, REGINA, p. 81
Cohnstaedt, *Western Canada 1909: Travel Letters by William Cohnstaedt*, p. 8.

COLLEGE BUILDING, UNIVERSITY OF SASKATCHEWAN, SASKATOON, p. 84
Walter C. Murray in Kerr, 'Building the University of Saskatchewan 1907–1930', p. 165.

GOVERNMENT HOUSE, REGINA, p. 87
John A. Macdonald, 1888, in Brennan, *Regina Before Yesterday: A Visual History 1882 to 1945*, p. 31.

Nicholas Flood Davin, Canada, House of Commons *Debates*, 20 July 1894, p. 6,494.

BIBLIOGRAPHY

Books, Reports, and Pamphlets

Baran, Anna Maria, *Ukrainian Catholic Churches of Saskatchewan* (Saskatoon: Modern Press, 1977).

Bodnar, Diana, 'The Three Prairie Legislative Buildings', *Prairie Forum: Special Issue on Prairie Architecture*, edited by Trevor Boddy, Vol. 5, No. 2, Fall 1980.

Boon, T. C. B., *The Anglican Church From the Bay to the Rockies* (Toronto: Ryerson Press, 1962).

Brennan, William J., ed. and intro., *Regina Before Yesterday* (Regina: 75th Anniversary Management Board, City of Regina, 1978).

Burley, David and David Myer, *Nipawin Reservoir Heritage Study, Vol. 3: Regional Overview and Research Considerations*, Saskatchewan Research Council Publication No. C-805-25-E-82, April 1982.

Canadian Encyclopedia, Vols. 1–3 (Edmonton: Hurtig Publishers, 1985).

Carter, Sarah, 'Material Culture and the W. R. Motherwell Home', *Prairie Forum*, Vol. 8, No. 1, Spring 1983.

Christensen, Deanna, *'A Convenient Place': A History of Fort Carlton, 1810–1885*, prepared for the Historic Parks Program, Parks Branch, Saskatchewan Parks and Renewable Resources, 1981.

– *Selected Aspects of Fort Pitt's History*, prepared for the Historic Parks Program, Parks Branch, Saskatchewan Parks and Renewable Resources, 1984.

City of Regina, Planning Department, *Heritage Tours*.

Cohnstaedt, Wilhelm, *Western Canada 1909: Travel Letters by Wilhelm Cohnstaedt*, translated by Herta Holle-Scherer, edited by Klaus H. Burmeister, Canadian Plains Studies No. 7, Canadian Plains Research Center, University of Regina, 1976.

Cowie, Isaac, *The Company of Adventurers* (Toronto: William Briggs, 1913).

Denny, Cecil E., *The Law Marches West* (Toronto: J. M. Dent Canada, 1939).

Eaglesham, Isabelle, *The Big Muddy Valley*, compiled for Saskatchewan History and Folklore Society, 1970.

Epp, H. T. and L. Townley-Smith, eds., *The Great Sand Hills of Saskatchewan: A Report Prepared for the Saskatchewan Department of the Environment and the Ecology and Archaeology and on Resource Management and Land Use in the Great Sand Hills of Saskatchewan*, March 1980.

Gillespie, Beryl C., 'Territorial Expansion of the Chipewyan in the 18th Century', *Proceedings: Northern Athapaskan Conference, 1971*, Vol. 2, edited by A. McFadyen Clark, Canadian Ethnology Service Paper No. 27, National Man Mercury Series, 1975.

Goldring, Philip, 'Whisky, Horses and Death: The Cypress Hills Massacre and Its Sequel', *Canadian Historic Sites: Occasional Papers in Archaeology and History No. 21*, Parks Canada, 1979.

Harmon, Daniel Williams, *A Journal of Voyages and Travels in the Interior of North America*, edited by Daniel Haskel with an introduction by W. L. Grant (Toronto: Courier Press, 1911).

– *Sixteen Years in the Indian Country: The Journal of Daniel Williams Harmon, 1800–1816*, edited with an introduction by W. Kaye Lamb (Toronto: Macmillan, 1957).

Hearne, Samuel, *A Journey From Prince of Wales Fort in Hudson's Bay to the Northern Ocean . . . in the Years 1769, 1770, 1771 and 1772*, edited with an introduction by Richard Glover (Toronto: Macmillan, 1958).

Hearne, Samuel and Philip Turnor, *Journals of Samuel Hearne and Philip Turnor Between the Years 1774 and 1792*, edited with an introduction by J. B. Tyrrell, Champlain Society, Toronto, No. 21, 1934.

Henry, Alexander, *Journal of Alexander Henry*, 28 & 29 August 1808, MG19, A13, Vol. 1, Public Archives of Canada.

Hind, Henry Youle, *Narrative of the Canadian Red River Exploring Expedition of 1857 and of the Assiniboine and Saskatchewan Exploring Expedition of 1858*, Vol. 1 (London: Longman, Green, Longman, and Roberts, 1860).

Hines, John, *The Red Indians of the Plains: Thirty Years' Missionary Experience in the Saskatchewan* (London: Society for Promoting Christian Knowledge, 1915).

Hodern, Paul, *Something Ventured, Something Gained: Reminiscences of a Barr Colonist* (Saskatoon, 1978).

Humphrys, Ruth, 'The Becktons of Cannington Manor', *The Beaver*, Winter 1982.

Kaye, Vladimir J., *Early Ukrainian Settlements in Canada, 1895–1900: Dr. Josef Oleskow's Role in the Settlement of the Canadian Northwest*, Ukrainian Canadian Research Foundation (Toronto: University of Toronto Press, 1964).

Kerr, Don, 'Building the University of Saskatchewan, 1907–1930', *Prairie Forum: Special Issue on Prairie Architecture*, edited by Trevor Boddy, Vol. 5, No. 2, Fall 1980.

Kerr, Don and Stan Hanson, *Saskatoon: The First Half-Century* (Edmonton, NeWest, 1982).

Klimko, Olga, *Preliminary Archaeological Investigations at the Marr Residence (326-11th Street, Saskatoon, Saskatchewan)*, Saskatchewan Research Council, SRC Publication No. C-805-53-E-81, November 1981.

Knight, Leith, *All the Moose... All the Jaw* (Moose Jaw 100, 1982).

Korvemaker, E. Frank, *Holy Trinity Anglican Church, Stanley Mission*, Historic Conservation, Saskatchewan Culture and Recreation, 1982).

McDougall, John, *Forest, Lake and Prairie: Twenty Years of Frontier Life in Western Canada, 1842–62* (Toronto: William Briggs, 1895).

– *Pathfinding on Plains and Prairies* (Toronto: William Briggs, 1895).

M'Gillivray, Duncan, *The Journal of Duncan M'Gillivray of the North West Company*, edited with an introduction by A. S. Morton (Toronto: Macmillan, 1929).

Mackenzie, Alexander, *Voyages From Montreal on the River St. Laurence Through the Continent of North America to the Frozen and Pacific Oceans in the Years 1789 and 1793...* (Toronto: Radisson Society of Canada, 1927).

Macoun, John, *Manitoba and the Great North West* (Guelph: World Publishing, 1882).

– *Sessional Papers*, Department of the Interior Annual Report, No. 3, 1881.

McWilliams, James, *A Walking Tour of Downtown Moose Jaw, 1982*, prepared for the Moose Jaw Art Museum and National Exhibition Centre, City of Moose Jaw.

Morice, A. G., *History of the Catholic Church in Western Canada* (Toronto: Musson Book Company, 1910).

Morris, Alexander, *The Treaties of Canada With the Indians* (Toronto: Facsimile reprint by Coles Publishing, 1979).

Morton, Desmond, *The Last War Drum: The North West Campaign of 1885* (Toronto: Hakkert, 1972).

Motherwell, W. R., 'Women's Present-Day Responsibilities', Reports of the Six Annual Conventions of the Homemakers Club of Saskatchewan (Saskatoon, 1916).

North-West Mounted Police, *Opening Up the West, Being the Official Reports to Parliament of the Activities of the Royal* [sic] *North-West Mounted Police Force From 1874–1881...*, introduction by Commissioner W. L. Higgitt, RCMP (Toronto: facsimile edition published by Coles Publishing, 1973; original published 1874–81).

Parks Canada, *Batoche National Historical Park* (booklet), 1984.

– *Guide to National and Historic Parks/Sites in Western and Northern Canada*, 1983.

– *W. R. Motherwell Homestead National Historic Park* (pamphlet), 1983.

Piniuta, Harry, trans., *Land of Pain, Land of Promise: First Person Accounts by Ukrainian Pioneers 1891–1914* (Saskatoon: Western Producer Prairie Books, 1978).

Peel, Bruce, *Steamboats on the Saskatchewan* (Saskatoon: Prairie Books, The Western Producer, 1972).

Rosenberg, Norman, *Edenbridge: The Memory Lives...* (Melfort: Phillips Publishers, 1980).

Rostecki, R. R., *The Early Court Houses of Saskatchewan*, Manuscript Report Series, 306, Parks Canada, 1977.

St. John, Mrs. Seward T., 'Diary, March 30–December 25, 1902', *Saskatchewan History*, Vol. 2, No. 2, Spring 1949.

– 'Diary, January 2, 1903–March 30, 1904', *Saskatchewan History*, Vol. 2, No. 3, Autumn 1949.

Saskatchewan Culture and Youth, *The Cypress Hills: A Natural History*, Museum of Natural History, Popular Series 15, n.d.

Saskatchewan Diamond Jubilee & Canada Centennial Corporation, *Guide to Historic Sites and Points of Interest* (1965).

Saskatchewan Parks and Renewable Resources pamphlets, *Cannington Manor, Holy Trinity—Stanley Mission, St. Victor's Petroglyphs* (1985).

Smith, J. G. E. 'The Ecological Basis of Chipewyan Socio-Territorial Organization', *Proceedings: Northern Athapaskan Conference, 1971*, Vol. 2, Canadian Ethnology Service Paper No. 27, National Museum of Man Mercury Series, 1975.

Spry, Irene M., ed., *The Papers of the Palliser Expedition, 1857–1860* (Toronto: The Champlain Society, 1968).

Stanley, G. F. G., 'Gabriel Dumont's Account of the North West Rebellion, 1885', *Canadian Historical Review*, Vol. 30, 1949.

Steele, Samuel B., *Forty Years in Canada* (Toronto: McGraw-Hill Ryerson, The Ryerson Archive Series, reissued, 1972).

Storm, Hyemeyohsts, *Seven Arrows* (New York: Ballantine Books, 1973).

Tarasoff, Koozma J., *Plakun Trava: The Doukhobors* (Grand Forks, B.C.: Mir Publication Society, 1982).

Turner, John Peter, *The North-West Mounted Police, 1873–1893*, Vols. 1 and 2 (Ottawa: King's Printer and Controller of Stationery, 1950).

Archival Sources

City of Regina, Planning Department

Glenbow-Alberta Institute Archives

Hudson's Bay Company Archives, Provincial Archives of Manitoba

Public Archives of Canada

Regina Public Library, Prairie History Room

Saskatchewan Archives Board

Saskatchewan Culture and Recreation, Museum of Natural History

Saskatchewan Legislative Library

Saskatchewan Parks and Renewable Resources, Parks Branch

Saskatchewan Power Corporation

Saskatchewan Research Council, Environment Sector

Saskatchewan Supply and Services, Central Survey and Mapping Agency

3